BIBLES, BEAVERS, AND BIG TIMBER

A FORESTER LOOKS FOR GOD IN THE WOODS

Bradley W. Antill

"It was always a dream of mine to work in the woods.
Be careful what you dream about."

©Bradley W. Antill 2008
No part of this book may be reproduced in any form whether mechanical, electronically, audio, or in any other way without the written permission of the publisher or author.

Edit revision 2019

ISBN   978-1-935298-05-2

Truth Publishers
Franklin, Illinois 62638
www.truthbookpublisher.com

All scripture quoted comes from NKJV

I would like to give a word of thanks to my Sunday school class at Lake Gaston Baptist Church for putting up with so many of my illustrations.

And a word of encouragement to the many folks at the Union Rescue Mission of Roanoke Rapids, North Carolina, where dreams and reality are often in great conflict; yet hope remains.

But mostly I give thanks to my wife, Cindy. She prays for me in the swamp.

Contents

Introduction	5
The Forester Is in the Woods!	7
Hello, Briars. Good-bye Clothes!	9
The Tree of the Tract	15
Legacy of the Nursery	19
A Hot Day in the Woods!!	22
Follow Your Compassman	26
Lean on Me	29
Logging for the Lord	32
Persistence or Long-suffering?	36
Dams and Damnation	40
Culverts	43
Follow the River	46
Stump Holes	51
Road Building 101	56
Logging and Lepers	59
Knots	63
Identity Theft	69
Standing	72
Salvage	77
Games	80
Let's Take a Cruise	83
Cypress Ponds	89
Food Piles	92
Image	95
Foresters and Fishing	99
Marking the Boundaries	103
The Pickle Bucket of Grace	107
The Ride Home	112

INTRODUCTION

I have been contemplating writing this book for a long time. It has been my heart's desire to share how the hand of God is manifested each day in my life, as well as how it is in yours. If God has indeed called me to be a forester, then He must be involved in my daily life, revealing Himself in and through the tasks I perform as I go about my days. As a pastor might spend his day pouring over the Scriptures, as is his calling, then a pipe welder, truck driver, or anyone obeying the call of God as to their daily vocation, must have the ability to see God daily also. It would hardly make sense for God to "shoo" His children away for a day. Imagine Joseph in the carpenter shop. Little Jesus sitting on a bench asks to help, but He, like any child, must be taught. The hands that molded the mountains, and fashioned the trees, must learn to shape a log into a board, and the board into a piece of furniture.

That sounds like a description of God working in our lives. How rough we are at the beginning. Bark covers us. Limbs protrude everywhere. But then along comes the woodcutter and down goes the tree. Across the grain goes the saw, and a log is produced. Again the coarse saw grinds away at the fibers of the log, and sawdust covers the floor; but through the dust and sweat, a board is created. The skilled carpenter applies his knowledge to the board—pressure here, a tack there, bending a little, trimming a little, and carving a little. Soon an idea begins to take shape. The wood is no longer a large unyielding tree, or a gangly log, but now....

a violin, a piano, a chair, a table.

Oh, to be crafted by God, and used for His glory, but Oh, the possible pain.

To be in the carpenter's hands can be frightening. There can be uncertainty and doubt. There can be pain from the pressure, the bending, the trimming, and the carving.

Maybe life on the stump is better. But then the only time the tree will make noise on its own is when it falls. No sweet melodious sound that will be, just a deafening crash followed by silence. A crude bench is all that will be created by the prostrate tree as it stretches its branches across the ground, embracing the earth it for so long sought to rise above. Such a bench serves only two purposes in the woods. One is a buffet for the local insect population. Every beetle, worm, termite, and ant nearby knows that "dinner is served" when a tree falls in the forest.

Another use of a fallen tree in the forest is rather unappealing. Those who have spent time in the woods have experienced it. Fallen trees are places where the furry creatures of the forest like to leave their scent. Think about how this is done, and you get the picture. Fox, bobcat, squirrel, or raccoon— they love to get off the ground and do things that create an odor. That is not how I want to end up, like that crude bench. Apply the axe, Lord, and bring on the saw. Sure, making sawdust may be painful, and the planer and sander scratch; but Oh for the finished product!

You see life is not about what we do, but about what we let God do with us. The Bible tells us in Revelation 4:11 that we were created for His pleasure, to give glory and honor to Him.

Come along with me to the woods. That place where over and over God has shown me examples and illustrations of who He is, and who I am supposed to be. Be prepared to get muddy, so you will need to take boots. We'll also need a compass, and definitely some bug spray. Working in the woods is not easy, and neither is life.

The Forester Is in the Woods!

Let's begin with some Biblical history. The first land management forester was Adam. God gave him the task of looking after the trees in the garden. The first procurement forester mentioned was Noah. God told him to go build an ark out of gopher wood, and that is exactly what a procurement forester does— "go for wood." Gideon was a logger. He cut down the idol groves of his father. Solomon built the temple using the cedars of Lebanon, and Asaph, according to Nehemiah, was the keeper of the king's forest. Amos worked with sycamore trees. Zacchaeus climbed a tree. Christ was crucified on one.

It would appear that since day six of Creation, trees have been involved daily in our lives. Over half of the wood harvested in the world is still used to provide heating and for use in cooking fires. The paper in this book comes from trees. Our houses are framed in wood, and our offices are trimmed in wood. Let's face it, without wood we would be in a world of hurt! Ever try to hang a picture on a rock wall?

I have always felt that God called me to the life and working profession of a forester. Ever since I sent for an USFS pamphlet entitled, "So You Want to Become a Forester," from the back of an outdoors magazine, I have followed that call. That was back in the eighth grade. While the following years brought thoughts of other professional callings, they were never clear, never distinct. So here I am.

The forester is truly a "jack-of-all-trades." On any given day, he or she might be working as a paralegal in the local courthouse searching out ownerships for tracts of land; or they are carrying a burning torch across a cutover in order to complete a prescribed burn, appraising timber, talking to school children, writing reports, downloading coordinates from GPS satellites, setting up logging operations, marking out roads, surveying, planting, or working with wildlife. That is just to name a few.

It is across this broad range of experiences that God works in my life. If I don't pay attention, I might miss it. Perhaps the hardest lessons to see are the ones that come on those ugly days, those days when you can think of several other more important, and certainly more enjoyable things that need to be done. But duty demands that the particularly unpleasant chores be accomplished.

In Colossians 3:23, Paul writes:

And whatever you do, do it heartily, as to the Lord and not to men...

While it is certainly true that a minister's vocation would seem like a full time calling, it is just as true that all believers are to live every day in Christ. Lives would certainly change if we put into serious practice what it says in Philippians 1:21:

For to me, to live is Christ, and to die is gain.

What an impact we could make, if we Christians would realize that whatever God has called us to do will have the same potential to affect lives as do missionaries, pastors, or other full time Christian vocations. We could learn so much more about God. Sounds like an adventure to me!

Hello, Briars. Good-bye Clothes!

The sale flyer advertised sixty acres of mature pine saw timber for sale. That's good. It sells at sealed bid, and that's good. The tract of land holding this desirable timber is in Horry County, South Carolina. That is a cause for concern. Some counties in the South have reputations for underbrush. Actually, underbrush does not do justice to describing the forests in the South. We are talking about walls of plant growth so thick that you seldom truly touch the ground. Let's talk about briars, vines of thin green aircraft cable with curled cat claws on every square inch. A landowner in Horry County would "pre-log" his timber before he put it up for sale. By this, I mean they would go in and log all of the pulpwood out, leaving only saw timber trees. This was usually done to open up the stand, thus making the remaining saw timber trees easier to measure and to appraise. However, if markets weren't good, he would let this block sit for a summer.

Think "nature abhors a vacuum." We arrive at the tract to see a green carpet, chest high, of razor-sharp briars. The pine trees are there, and they are excellent. But now we have to "fall out" of the truck and measure them, fighting briars all the way. The enjoyment of the timber is quickly removed by the pain of the briars ripping holes in our shirts, pants, skin—you get the picture. You can preach several sermons about being in a briar patch; certainly, one on controlling your tongue.

But let's look at the dirt. From the size of the trees, we might guess their age to be sixty years. Thus sixty years ago, this particular tract was harvested, and pine trees started to grow from seed sources that fell on the ground or were planted. At that point, it became a race, a race for sunlight, for minerals, and for water. The pines were competing with other trees, but in particular against the briars. Briars seem to grow everywhere, as if the very soil has the ability to spontaneously produce them in the absence of seeds. They grow thick. They entangle everything they touch. They absorb the sunlight meant for the seedlings. They absorb the water meant for the roots of the seedlings, and finally they wrap themselves around the seedling in an attempt to strangle the very life out of it.

In Matthew 13, Jesus talks about just such a scene. Seeds are being sown. As these seeds hit the ground, things begin to happen. Verse 7 says, *"And some fell among thorns, and the thorns sprang up and choked them."* In verse 22 Jesus explains that these thorns represent the *"cares of this world"* that choke the plant so that it produces no fruit. Lesson number one to be learned from the briar patch is watch out for the "cares of this world." These "cares" are subtle at first, scattered throughout your life. They hide in our desire to have a bigger house or fancier car, the desire to have more money in the bank or another relationship. These desires quickly grow when given the attention they crave. The seeds of fame blossom as we yearn for the next promotion or to win another trophy.

While some of those things and countless other activities are not essentially bad, they are when they begin to take over our life. Our time in pursuing them is consumed first, then our energy. Twenty years later, we look back at what was once a thriving young "forest of a life" and all we see are briars. A marriage is in shambles. We do not recognize our kids. Ulcers are common, as is dissatisfaction. Sleepless nights become the norm. What happened? We started to like the briar patch. We got used to the thorns. We overlooked the rips and tears and the blood.

To cruise such a stand of timber is the duty of the forester. The unpleasant aspect of the briars must be dealt with or endured—just like life. We have to go into the world, but this time, make it hurt. If you have to spend time away from your family, feel the hurt, because that's a briar. Don't get used to it. Think of the time you are missing back at home or at church. These opportunities come to us once in life: time to be with your kids, to play catch or go fishing, to eat supper with your wife, to visit a friend who is sick, to work with youth showing them God's promises. The essence of the briar patch is time. Don't get caught in it. It wants all of your time, and therefore all of you. Let God set the priorities in your life, and you will be amazed at the lack of briar patches you run into.

The second lesson to be learned from the briar patch is one of perseverance. The good forester will complete the cruise regardless of the obstacles presented by the briars. After all, timber like this is a rare and precious commodity. And how did the trees get to be like this? They are tall, with a larger than average diameter, good form, and well crowned. Look in the dictionary under "perfect saw timber tree," and you will see their picture. But how did they grow in this briar patch? How did they keep from getting choked and pulled down by the vines all around them? It was persistence; they established their roots first, strong roots that gave them a foundation to compete with the briars. Strong roots that gave them energy to push through the clutter of vines and briars. As they grew higher than the surrounding plants, they began to grow even faster, racing away from the clutter. Yet they also began to create shade. Briars hate shade. Briars slowly sink away as shade comes in. Only the strong seedlings survive, the seedlings that stay at it, develop roots, and grow towards the light.

Our relationships, especially with God, work that way. It is all based upon the foundation. Remember that song from Sunday school when you were a youth? Sing with me, "The foolish man built his house upon the sand…" Well, some of us had best just hum it until we are in the shower or in the car—alone. The song tells the same parable that Jesus taught in Matthew 7:24-27. Two builders used different foundations. One used sand, the other rock. Then the storms came. Storms are often the pressures of life. They are not always big and dramatic, like a trip to the emergency room. Sometimes they are seemingly harmless at the time, such as: a new secretary, a promotion, perhaps a chance to play ball, or a night on the road away from the family. Be assured, they are storms. Like the briars, they will attach, pull, absorb, and fight your every step. Jesus tells His followers that to be considered wise, to have a foundation that is able to withstand the pressure storms of life, we have to do something. Do you see it in the beginning of verse 24?

There are two steps, hearing and doing. We have to hear what Jesus is telling us, and then we have to do what He directs. Hearing anything in a briar patch is tough. The briars are scratching at your clothes, words are forming on your lips, and the vines are shaking the surrounding brush.

But Christ is still calling, and we could hear what He says if we but pause to listen:

"...unless one is born again, he cannot see the kingdom of God." (John 3:3b).

"But seek first the kingdom of God and His righteousness, and all these things shall be added to you." (Matthew 6:33).

"...I am the resurrection and the life. He who believes in Me, though he may die, he shall live." (John 11:25).

We can all listen. Imagine your son is sitting in the den, reading his favorite book. A shrill sound erupts from the living room. The smoke alarm! The smell of smoke reaches your nostrils as you bolt from the couch to see the kitchen in flames. Your wife and daughter meet you at the front door and out onto the lawn you go. You call the fire department with your cell phone. You look around. Where's your son? He was in the den reading. It was quiet in there; he had to have heard the smoke alarm. He had to have heard you screaming to get out of the house. The den has a huge patio door; all he has to do is walk out! You race around the blazing house, straining to see inside the den, and there he sits, still reading. Even outside you can hear the sirens. Is he deaf? You race to the door, pushing it open and scream at him. Slowly he lifts his head, looking at you with a quizzical stare and says, "Is that our smoke alarm?"

Listening doesn't guarantee action, or even response. We first have to be convinced that the words being spoken are indeed for us. You cannot give a man "direction" until he is convinced, he is lost. (And the women say, "Amen!"). We will never accept the words of Christ, until we realize that they are for us. The very One who created us, who loves us, who holds the very life we have in His nail-scarred hands, has life-giving and sustaining information for us. He knows the way out of the briar patch. Hear the words that Jesus has for you, and then apply them. "Just do it," as the slogan says. You can't deny the brambles are out there, but why let them leave you in shambles.

Now often in the forestry business, there seems to be a clear disconnect between the field side of the business and the office side. This group is often affectionately called the "accountants." Readers who are accountants are probably asking the question, "Why even go into the briar patch at all?" They do not understand that a Carolina Bay is a pocket of brush so thick that it is nearly impossible to penetrate on foot. At times, nothing short of a D-5 bulldozer, or a ground hive of yellow jackets will propel a forester through it.

Several years ago, the story was reported of a criminal fleeing from the police. He left his car and fled on foot into a Carolina bay in southeastern North Carolina. Local law enforcement refused to follow him. They stated quite confidently that he would come back. They were right. After one night, he stumbled out of the bay into the arresting arms of the officers. His clothes were in shreds. He was bleeding, and he had encountered several "creature discomforts" while in the brush: mosquitoes, snakes, ticks, yellow flies. These bays, scattered throughout the coastal south, are given such names as "Hell," "Purgatory," and "Hell's Half Acre." You get the point. Unfortunately, some of these bays actually hold timber, thus there are times when the only option is to enter the briar patch and appraise the trees.

The good news is there are things we can do to make it easier. Of course, a D-5 bulldozer is a good choice, and truthfully this is often done, allowing the tractor to make access paths to the timber. But another choice that exists is special clothing items such as briar pants and briar jackets, which are akin to heavy leather from a local Harley gang, or maybe a suit of armor from a local history museum. These items do help even though they are not always the best options on days when the local weatherman strongly suggests, no work should be done outside, because of the heat index.

Paul makes a similar suggestion in Ephesians 6:11, where he advises us to *"put on the whole armor of God"*. If ever a briar patch is described, it is described in verse 12 where the word "wrestle" is used to describe our struggles against Satan. The aim of our enemy is to defeat us, entangle us, strangle us, and to make us bleed. We are admonished to take truth, righteousness, the gospel, faith, salvation, and the "Sword of the Spirit," (the Word of God), into the battle with us.

Briar patches are all around us. Some we mistakenly jump into only to find ourselves entangled and helpless. Bleeding and in pain, we long for the open fields of life. We seem to see it just ahead, but we cannot struggle against the briars to make it there. Some patches we have to go through; it is a part of our journey. Wear the right clothing. If you don't, you and your wardrobe will be in sad need of repair when the day is finally over. In Matthew 11:28, Jesus calls to those of us in the briar patches of life. We are tired. We want out. It is never fun to go through a briar patch alone. Take someone along with you and it will surely change the day, especially if that someone is a big strapping fellow armed with a machete and a desire to make a hole. Perhaps, when God made the briar patches, he did not intend for us to tear through them alone. Jesus longs to go with us, to be beside us, to encourage us, to break a path, and to protect us from those briars. After all, he wore a crown of thorns because He loves you; because he doesn't want you to spend a day, a night, or your entire life entangled in the briar patch.

"Come to Me" He says so softly in verse 28. Can you hear Him? Can you stop for just a moment and hear His call? *"Come to me...and I will give you rest"*. That is a promise from the briar patch.

The Tree of the Tract

For those of you not familiar with the timber industry, a few words of explanation may help concerning this chapter. First the basics:

Lumber is made out of wood, as is paper.

Wood comes from trees.

Before they can become useable, trees must be cut down (logged).

Trees are property, and therefore must be purchased.

From this point on it is simple economics. A landowner has a tract of timber that is large enough to be logged. He then lets that fact be known, and soon foresters trying to buy the timber will show up like ants at a picnic. The successful buyer will have the timber logged, and the timber will be delivered to a manufacturing facility called a mill, to be cut into boards, sliced for panels, or dissolved to make paper. The process of evaluating the tract of timber varies from experienced guesses to scientific guesses. In the end, the boldest guesser wins. (Unless the solid trees he bought turn out to be hollow when they hit the ground; in which case he loses, and the other foresters who lost become the winners!) Understand? If so, please send me a note and explain it to me.

Let's take an imaginary trip to Mr. Smith's farm where there are forty acres of timber to sell. Now upon arrival, we have to determine what it is about Mr. Smith's timber that makes us want to risk our money. We evaluate the ground. It's good ground, but in the wet season, it may not support logging activity. Mark it down as average. We evaluate the access. The log trucks will have to cross a field of soybeans. That is typical, so let's mark it average. We evaluate the timber species. It has a good mixture of hardwood and softwood. Mark it average. Three averages are worth further investigation, so we begin the cruise. The cruise is the scientific guessing method employed by foresters, but defined by the aforementioned

BIBLES, BEAVERS, AND BIG TIMBER

"accountants" as being an exact science. The forester writes on his appraisal that he has purchased 2,000 tons of saw timber. He knows this is a guess because the weights of the trees are not truly known until they are cut down and weighed. He will be happy with 1,800 tons and ecstatic with anything higher than 1,800. The accountant wants and expects 2,000 tons. In truth, the carnival barker would be a good timber cruiser— "Hello Mr. Red Oak, looks like you weigh 1,900 pounds, step up on the scale and win a prize!"

It is while cruising the tract that the quality of the timber is noticed in detail—how many trees there are, how tall, where they are located, etc. Then you see it. It is beautiful. It would seem like light is shining on it from above. The mosquitoes have stopped swarming you, the sweat has suddenly dried on your face, and you behold it— "the tree of the tract." It is the perfect tree, just the right diameter, tall, with no defects. It is the type of tree that will make perfect, knot-free lumber.

You can imagine the cheers from the sawyer at the mill as he slaps you on the back in congratulations. In your imagination you become the forester in the story told over and over again by the salesman who sold the perfect lumber from your perfect tree. Having found such a tree, you immediately look for evidence whether other foresters have found this rare treasure. You mark the spot with your GPS so that you can bring your boss back to see it. After all, this tract now becomes special. No more is it average. It will demand a sacrifice from the "accountants" to give more money to insure the purchase of the timber from Mr. Smith. You want that tree. As a forester, you have seen a lot of trees, and there is rarely a perfect tree. Often the outside looks good but the inside has worms, or the growth rings are too wide, or the heart is off center. Therefore to find a "tree of the tract," to see it in the woods having survived the hardships of nature, including termites and woodpeckers, is special.

Jesus tells us a parable about such a thing. It is located in Matthew 13:45-46. In the parable a merchantman seeking rare pearls comes across the perfect pearl, and selling all that he has, he takes the money and buys the perfect pearl. It had value to him beyond the normal, so much so that he gave up all to obtain it. Have you ever come across something that you were willing to give up everything in order to obtain it? You want a promotion so you gave up your family. You crave more adventure, so you gave up your marriage. You desired more money in the bank, so you gave up your health and became a workaholic. We are faced with this dilemma daily. Do we consider eternity?

In the parable, Jesus is talking about Heaven. Heaven is the rare pearl, the "tree of the tract." That special possession is worth giving up all we have in order to gain its possession. There's the rub, giving up something. Since I was a kid, I have known how to say "Mine!" And I say it well, with feeling and conviction. But Heaven sounds like a good place to spend eternity. What do I have to give up, or how much money will it cost me?

Here's the good part, the price has already been paid. Jesus went to the cross to pay for it. He gave the ultimate sacrifice to make Heaven available to you and me. But we have to accept it. The pearl is being offered to us. Mr. Smith is giving us the tree. Do you want it? Do you want to live eternally with Jesus? We all would say, "Yes," but we still hesitate to take the gift. We know it will cost us something, and it is really all we have to offer--our lives. This is done not in some feat of human sacrifice, but in submission. It comes when we relinquish ourselves to Christ, to say, "Yours," and not "Mine."

Mark 8:36-37 *"For what will it profit a man if he gains the whole world, and loses his own soul? Or what will a man give in exchange for his soul?"*

Compared to eternal life, how can anything else add up? Is my job or my relationships or my possessions of greater value than eternity? The old story about hitching the U-Haul to the hearse is funny, but sadly true. When I stand before God a split nanosecond after I die, He will ask me one question. He will accept only one answer. "Did you accept the gift of My Son?" To put it another way, "Did you give up what you cannot keep, in order to gain that which you could not lose?"

I can thankfully say, "Yes." As a young child at a Sunday morning church service, I walked down to the preacher and told him I wanted to go to Heaven. He had a man show me in the Bible that Jesus died for my sins. He showed me Romans 6:23, *For the wages of sin is death, but the gift of God is eternal life in Jesus Christ our Lord.* And Romans 10:9, *...that if you confess with your mouth the Lord Jesus and believe in your heart that God has raised Him from the dead, you will be saved.*

Jesus died on a tree, a cruel cross, for my sins and yours. Where does that tree rate with you? You are not wandering through the forest, blindly walking past the "tree of the tract," are you?

The Legacy of the Nursery

Some of you men, as well as some of the women, might be wondering about this chapter. You might be asking yourself, "How does being in the woods tie into being in the nursery?" Because isn't it true that if the kids have the crud, dad heads for the woods? Or if it's hunting season, then dad is in the woods instead of at home helping with the kids. Well, those may be applied here in some manner; but for now, the nursery in this context is where seedlings are grown for planting. Yes, hundreds of thousands of little one-year-old seedlings carefully grown, only to be uprooted, wrapped in paper bags and put in the refrigerator. Next is a bumpy ride across some half-frozen, muddy road. Then they are tossed to the ground to be repacked in a canvas bag. Finally, they are taken and shoved into a mere slit in the ground, and there they will forever stay until they are eventually harvested—or eaten!

Before we go any further, let's go back to the beginning of the life of a tree. To grow a tree, you need a seed. Now for some folks, any old seed may do, but not you the forester. You want trees that are fast growing, able to spring into action and provide shade, food, or income. Furthermore, you want one that is going to be healthy and able to resist disease and stress. The place to go to get such a tree is a nursery. There scientists have been carefully gathering seeds: not just any seeds, good seeds from the biggest and strongest trees. Often these seeds are planted to produce a good tree with even more good seeds. I suppose you can get the picture that special trees are "cropped" so that the seeds they produce will in like fashion produce a tree somewhat like the parent tree. Many techniques are used in the nursery, but the goal is the same—get good seeds from good trees.

Now if you were a tree, there are certain traits you would want to pass on to your offspring. You need to be able to outgrow the vegetative competition such as grass, weeds, and sweet gum trees. You need to be able to withstand periods of drought or periods of high water. You would have to have the ability to grow fast into the upper canopy to maximize photosynthesis and to bend with the wind and not break. After all, what kind of parent would want their "genetic material" to just fall to the ground and perish? Why that truly would be outrageous.

King David had just such a dilemma. He was getting old, and he knew it would soon be time to meet God face to face. He had made plans to hand his kingdom to his son Solomon, but even greater was his desire to make sure that Solomon followed after God as he had. Now David had certainly learned his lessons. From beating the local bully to being bug-eyed at a woman in a bathtub, David knew all about the highs and lows of life. What a source of wisdom.

In I Chronicles 22:11-19, we read that David encourages his son and gives him a goal. He calls upon God to supply the child with wisdom and understanding, as well as the ability to guide Israel. If you remember your Bible stories from Sunday school, a few years after this, after David had died, Solomon was given the opportunity to ask God for anything (II Chronicles 1). He asked for wisdom, and God abundantly supplied it. David had made an impression on his son as to the importance of wisdom.

David also gave Solomon a warning (I Chronicles 22:13). He was careful to point out to Solomon that following God required obedience. This was a lesson David had learned with much bitterness over the years. Obedience with God is not optional. At the end of this passage, in verse 19, David sends his son forth with instructions to seek the Lord and to work for His honor and glory.

What better gift can a child receive from a parent than to be given encouragement, instruction, and guidance in following God! You see we are all just like the trees in that nursery. If given the opportunity to produce children, then we have an awesome responsibility to see that they receive the best from us. Oh, we worry about passing on our acute business acumen, but do we work to make sure they are seeking the Lord? We show them how to bake a pie, take apart a carburetor, but can they use the Bible to seek answers for the questions of life? Of all the DNA and genetic material, of all the life lessons and experiences I have had, if I do not make absolutely sure that I have passed on to my children the ability to find and know Jesus, then I have done them a terrible disservice.

A Hot Day in the Woods!!

You know the expression— "It's not the heat, it's the humidity." Let's flashback to junior high school, and find our science class. The lesson is about the weather. Humidity, the amount of moisture in the air, is in fact a key element in how our bodies react to heat. Therefore, as humidity increases and heat increases, our bodies begin to feel the heat with more intensity.

Now, welcome back to the present and welcome to the South: land of heat and humidity. Blink and you will sweat. The kind of day I really love is the day the local news channel has issued an ozone alert. It goes like this: "The high heat and humidity will make it extremely dangerous to be outside today. Residents are advised to stay inside as much as possible." At that point, the boss-man laughs, and although he plans on following the weatherman's advice, he hands you a map and a job and sends you out the door. While there are certain advantages to getting up early and getting things done before the heat of the day arrives, sometimes you just have to face it head on.

Now on such a hot day, why would any critter want to wear a fur suit and swim around in a swamp infested by cottonmouth moccasins? I don't know either, but I am talking about beavers. They never seem to take a day, or month off. They are always working, always trying to get into that one pipe that will flood a road, or make a dam in just the right place to flood the timber you need to cut. Even on a hot day, the diligent—that's French for crazy—forester has to make the rounds to keep them out of those drainpipes and from flooding those precious timberlands.

One such day, as described above, I had to make several rounds in an effort to thwart some of those furry little engineers. And as the day progressed, I realized that I was not going to get all the rounds done before the hottest part of the day set in. No problem, I thought. I am young and in great shape. So while the melting clock on the dash of the truck read 1:30, and the temperature plus the humidity pushed 110 degrees, and the local "DJ" was saying, "Don't go out there" —I did. Now my preferred mosquito repellent is 100% cotton; that is, I wear a long sleeve shirt. It actually keeps bugs and poison ivy off of my arms, and for that I endure the added heat. On this day I dressed as I usually do, long sleeve shirt and hip waders, and into the swamp I plunged.

The problem on this particular tract was this: beavers were damming a stream under a power line about a half-mile into the tract. We were scheduled to log this tract, so the water had to go; therefore the beavers had to go. I had to check that my recent trapping activities had been successful, and that in fact, the water level had dropped so that we could move a logger onto the tract. It is here that the wildlife management portion of my college degree was finally used! Because of the nature of the land, and the activities of the beaver, the entire trip in was knee deep in mud. I hope you can get a picture of all of this, especially the young man (me) who thought he could handle the heat. He was unconcerned about it. He never even thought about it. Just as arrogant and confident of his abilities as he could be. But with each step, each herculean effort to pull a boot out of the mud and set it back down, and each attempt to make another step towards the dry land that seemed miles away, his confidence was quickly eroding. It was on the trip back to the truck that certain ideas began to flash through his mind, such as:

"How will they find my body out here?"

"Would it be better to die suddenly with a heart attack or simply collapse and fall into the aforementioned moccasin ridden swamp?"

"Do mosquitoes still take your blood after you have already died?"

But as I stopped every few feet, trying to breathe and holding on to trees to keep from falling, I had a revelation: "A cup of water would sure taste good right now!"

BIBLES, BEAVERS, AND BIG TIMBER

In Psalms 143:6, David writes: *I spread out my hands to You; my soul longs for You like a thirsty land.* In Psalm 42:2, the writer declares; *My soul thirsts for God..."* David lived in the south, southern Israel that is, so heat and humidity was not uncommon for him. He experienced more than one hot day in the woods chasing sheep, and he gives us a great picture of why the Bible states that David was a man after God's own heart.

Extreme thirst, have you ever been there? Now I had every confidence that I would get back to my truck. I also knew that I was close to exploding into flames. The effort became more than just a walk. It took on emotion. A desire to get out of the heat and find something cool to drink came over me. David knew. When living in a desert, one learns to appreciate thirst for what it is. It is a warning that the body is getting too dry. Within the heat and the dryness is death. The body goes into shock, shuts down, and pulls the plug. How about some water? Life is in the water.

Every day is like a hot day in the woods. Every day brings with it the distant specter of death: a car out of control, a sudden heart attack, or just being at the wrong place at the wrong time. We have no guarantee that another day will be granted to us. Yet on we go. We ignore the radio, the warnings, the lessons we have learned. We dive into the swamp with all of its dangers. Those very things we rely upon to traverse the swamp, the shirts and the boots, are really adding to our discomfort. We have left behind the one item that will insure our survival--the water.

In John 4:14, Jesus is talking to a woman who is thirsty. She has come to the well to get some water. He tells her, *"...but whoever drinks of the water that I shall give him will never thirst. But the water that I shall give him will become in him a fountain of water springing up into everlasting life."* Christ is the answer to our thirst. The desire that we have within us for something we never seem to find. Some will try to fill the emptiness inside with a career. Others will seek to drink from sensual pleasure. Still others will try drugs and alcohol. Many try to just ignore the nagging thirst. They know it is there. It is a pesky feeling in the back of their mind. It picks at them whenever they see a baby or a starry night. Whenever a tree sheds an autumn leaf, or a friend dies, it is there. The mouth is dry. The soul is parched. There is the emotion that something is missing, and that something is critical to our survival.

Jesus Christ is our living water. David knew where to go to quench his thirst. The woman at the well, a woman whose personal life was in shambles, finally heard what she had been ignoring all her life—water gushing. The water that changed her life can change yours too. Are you out in the woods on a hot day? Thirsty? Do what David did and reach for the Lord. Reach for eternal life.

Follow Your Compassman

Whenever the need arises to cruise expensive timber or to cruise timber in rough terrain, the need for a partner arises. The two-man cruising team will usually divide the duties in half. One duty maneuvering across the property, making sure plots are taken at the correct locations. The other duty is measuring the plot. Getting there is often the hard part. The cruise usually begins at the office, where a map is drawn of the property, and then some sort of random plot sequence is laid out. These plots represent the points where data on the timber will be collected. To get there, the compassman lays out a bearing and a distance.

Now a lot of bad things can happen if you mess up on your map. For instance, your acreage may be off. How is this bad? Imagine your investigation of the tract determines the value of the timber to be $4,000 per acre, on thirty-eight acres. You do the math. If your competitor also finds there to be $4,000 per acre, in timber value, but correctly determines the tract to have forty acres, he will bid higher than you, and that is bad. Also, if the other fellow thought there was equal value, but the acreage was forty-four, then he will buy the timber. However, he will lose money. That is bad. The distribution of the sample can also be messed up, causing the cruisers to miss areas of the property that may hold a higher value of timber. The bottom line here is that the compassman has a responsibility to follow the map. In theory, he knows where he is going.

Now I have seen a compassman completely mess up a cruise. Some of the better messes were caused by heavy brush, ground bees, standing water, large ditches, power lines, and the ever popular "the metal plate in your head is throwing off my compass" excuse. You begin to doubt your compassman when you hear him mumbling things under his breath such as, "There's not supposed to be a river here," or "I know I have crossed that log before," or any such phrase that describes the heritage of the compass and its inventor in general.

There are also ways to follow a compassman. On any tract there will be areas of heavy brush, briars, and water. The compassman, rather than risk losing his bearing and distance, will usually have to keep his line straight through these obstacles. After he has ripped his way through such obstacles, you should follow. Showing up ten minutes later, having found an easier way around, will not endear you to him, and you will begin to find large branches being snapped in your direction.

The compassman must trust his compass, and here is the first lesson of the woods. Trust, I say again, trust your compass. I have had many a conversation with my compass, usually when I am "way back" in a swamp, and my compass is pointing in the wrong direction; or so I believed.

In Psalms 119, the psalmist writes verse after verse on the reliability of God's Word, comparing life to a journey and the Bible as our guide, or compass, if you will. Verse 101 speaks of restraining our feet from following evil, and verse 102 speaks of staying the course. Verse 104 describes God's Word as giving us an understanding of the right and wrong ways. It is *"...a lamp unto my feet and a light unto my path,"* proclaim verse 105. We consult it in times of confusion, in times when our path may be obscured. We consult it in times of gladness, when we are confident of our walk and path. But let the words and the prompting from the Bible disagree with what we perceive to be the right direction for our lives, and we have a problem. I have a book in my library entitled, * *Finding Your Way in the Outdoors.* On pages 156 and 157 is a listing of why navigational errors occur. Number five is mistrusting your compass, and instead relying on your senses. If my senses could be trusted, I would never need a compass. But it is true, we do not like things that disagree with our sense of what is right.

Not trusting your compass can cause bad things to happen. Of course, you can get lost. You waste time and energy, and cause others discomfort. You cost your company money, and if the local rescue squad has to leave a softball game to come and find you, watch out! Worst of all, you may even die. Why? Because you thought your

"Daniel Boone" sense-of-direction was better than the compass in your pocket. Mistrusting God's compass, His Word, can be truly bad. What happens? A divorce happens. Bitterness happens. A life of fear happens. Many sleepless nights happen. Hell for all eternity happens. These things are bad. The Bible is not a collection of old stories or a screenplay for Cecil B. It is the instruction manual for our lives. God has given us a great gift—the gift of life. He has given us a greater gift, His Son Jesus. Then He provided for us the instructions on how to put them both together.

While we are on the subject of trusting the compass, consider old Jonah. Now there was a fellow who clearly knew what God wanted him to do, but he had other plans. He decided that his way made more sense. So he ran, he slept, and then he swam. Talk about bad things. Being chum for a big fish is bad with a capital "B." I can see Ol' Jonah, shaking his compass, and then shaking his head. He's looking across the swamp saying, "No way, I am not supposed to go that way. That just won't do." So off he went. His senses told him to get on a boat and go to Joppa, while his compass pointed to Nineveh and a big tent meeting.

The question is where are you? Perhaps you are this very minute wrestling with what your senses are saying, seeking to deny the verses of the Bible and what God is saying. Like a compass needle, you keep spinning God's Word, trying to get it to change, but it won't. God's Word is truth, and truth never changes. When it says your sins will find you out, they will. When it says "flee lust," it means to run like the wind. When it warns you to be faithful, it is not kidding. Trust your compass. Trust the Compassman. After all He has nail scars in His hands.

Finding Your Way in the Outdoors, Robert L. Mooers, Jr.; Copyright Meredith Corporation 1990, Popular Science Books, Sedgewood Press

Lean on Me

I suppose you are thinking about someone singing in the woods after reading the title to this chapter. Well I do not make a habit of singing in the woods. I let the mosquitoes do that. However the song and the meaning of the song "Lean on Me" do have a place in the woods. Before we sing that chorus, let's head to the woods. At least there, if we break out into song, only the squirrels will hear us.

We are driving across the farmer's field, approaching his fifty acres of timber. The stand borders the field on two sides. As we approach the stand, we notice that the trees along the field are rather large, with lots of limbs, and the brush appears to be thick. The rookie forester believes he has wasted his time. His mill does not want such rough-looking logs, and he would rather not fight brush on such poor looking timber. But before we leave, let's look closer. The brush around the stand is indeed heavy, forming a fence-like barrier around the timber. There is a reason for this. The young forester will learn that sunlight coming in from the field edge is the cause. The morning or afternoon sunlight will angle its way into the stand, causing briars, saplings, honeysuckle, and a host of vegetation to grow. With a little persistence, the stand can be penetrated, and after some sixty to seventy feet, the stand will usually clear out under the timber. The shade from the interior trees will keep the forest floor shaded, and in doing so inhibit the growth of most shrubs and small trees.

Our young forester, after breaking past the exterior defense of the stand, now notices a change in the trees. They have become slightly smaller in diameter, but they have fewer limbs. It looks like a stand his mill would like to have. What has happened?

Trees on the outside of a stand, particularly one with a field edge, will always outgrow trees on the interior of a stand. It is simply a matter of sunlight and moisture. Trees on the edge have a whole side free of competition and all the sunlight they want, and all the water and nutrients they need. They don't have to share. For this reason they grow. But there is a drawback—limbs. As a tree grows, limbs serve the purpose of supplying more branches and thus more leaves. This results in more photosynthesis. Inside a stand, with other trees to compete with, the trees must grow upward as fast as they can to capture as much sunlight as possible. Branches, taking valuable nutrients away from the trunk, will slow the vertical growth down, causing a tree to lose its spot in the sunlight. The edge trees do not have this problem, as they already have sunlight. Thus they grow big old branches.

In short, the large trees and the brush serve as a barrier to the interior trees. When storms and high winds roar across the land this barrier of large trees and heavy underbrush absorb the initial blast. They form a barrier, protecting the inner trees from the full force of the gusting winds. This is especially evident when a hurricane comes ashore. When Hurricane Fran struck in 1996, stands of trees along the Coastal Plain of North Carolina took a severe beating, in particular, trees along the field edges. The gale force winds would rocket across the bare, open fields and slam into the woodlots. The pressure upon the trees to break was tremendous, and many did. But it was the squat trees, with their big branches, and the brush that took the full brunt of the storm. By the time the wind penetrated the stand, it had lost much of its fury. These barrier trees lost limbs, tops, and many of them fell inward. Some took on a fatal lean, but they had served their purpose. The higher quality timbers, the trees nestled inside the stand, were spared because the barrier trees were present.

The Apostle Paul wrote in Galatians 6:2

Bear one another's burdens, and so fulfill the law of Christ.

As a father, I can especially relate to the idea of protecting and bearing burdens for my children, shielding them from situations that may cause them harm. I would do this even at the expense of getting hurt myself. After all, that is my job. But Paul here states that Christ expects that same sacrifice for the sake of others, not just my kids. That's tough to do. Could I accept an insult that I don't deserve? Help to pay a bill I did not incur? Giving my hard earned money to help someone in need? Where would it stop? I notice Paul did not place a limit or qualifier on this verse, and that is scary. In the woods, the barrier trees offer protection until they rest on the forest floor. Their value, while maybe not in terms of grade lumber, is certainly in the protection of the higher-value, inner trees. Maybe Christ had that in mind when He admonished us to think about others first.

In Philippians 2: 3b and 4, Paul again is after us to look at others first, even to value their life and well-being over our own. He wrote:

...let each esteem others better than himself. Let each of you look out not only for his own interests, but also for the interests of others.

Our nature is to be the valued commodity, the fine saw-timber tree nestled within the safety of the forest, protected from the wind. Check your roots and look at your limbs. Maybe you have never had to struggle for a little sunlight or a little water. Maybe you have a place to claim on the outside of the stand. The Master is looking for a few stout-hearted followers, willing to stand in the wind, willing to take a blow.

Logging for the Lord

Let's talk about loggers. Are they hardworking? Absolutely, if they are successful, or want to be, they must be hardworking and then some. Must they be creative? Without a doubt, every tract, every change in the weather, every shift in mill needs, demand that the logger be able and ready to adapt. The mentality needed to be a successful logger has not changed for hundreds of years. Hit the woods early, work until dark, go home and work on the ax/saw/machines/trucks until it is time to hit the woods again. It often seems like an endless cycle, like a carpenter building the same house over and over again. But a logger, who is usually a third or fourth generation logger, sees each day as a new challenge. The daily challenge is to get the trees cut and loaded on the truck. Next, he must get the truck to the highway and then to the mill. Everything seems to go against their wishes each step along the way. The overnight rain that pleases the farmer causes a few more gray hairs on the head of the logger. Wet woods and a soggy road will not help him complete the cycle today. The equipment breakdowns seem to always come just when the operation is humming along. The truck breaks down or the highway gets clogged with traffic or the mill is closed. With so much that can go wrong, and so much that seems to go wrong, why does anyone stay in this trade?

Why would anyone want to cut down a tree in the first place? Perhaps we should look to the Scriptures for that one. Yep, logging is a time-honored trade, found in the pages of Holy Writ. Surprised? Shocked? Let me explain. Go to any society in the world, particularly if you went to them for the first time, i.e. as an explorer, and you would find they all have a religious system, and that system has a leader: maybe a medicine man, a witch doctor, a priest, or a pastor. Why is this true? Romans 1:19-20 explains that we were all created with the knowledge of God, an understanding that He exists, and of his expectations. Those same societies also have laws, amazingly similar to other societies. But something happened to our vision of God. It became polluted. We chaffed at the idea of being accountable to an all-knowing God, and decided to change the rules. Verses 21-23 explain that we decided to worship the created instead of the Creator. We decided that we would answer to our own "gods."

Here is where the trees came into play. Folks began to call trees by names, and bow down to them and talk to them. And if someone had a good day trading at the market, when he passed an oak tree, he would say a prayer to it in thanks. Sound crazy? No, it sounds sad. Read the papers and you will find folks chaining themselves to trees to protect them from the saw. These same folks try to explain their actions by telling us of the conversation they had with the tree in question just yesterday and how the spirit of the tree spoke to them. You might laugh at this, but it is way more serious than that. You see to some, the idea of a tree being a "spiritual being" is absurd, yet to others it is absolute truth.

In Old Testament times these "god trees" were usually found in small clumps called "groves." These groves were the family church so-to-speak. The nation of Israel found itself in a terrible fix. They ignored God for a long time and began worshipping idols. God allowed an enemy, the Midianites, to come in and abuse them. The people hid in fear of these Midianites. Then one day, God called on a fellow named Gideon, and a logger was born. It began under an oak tree, where according to Judges 6 an angel of the Lord spoke to Gideon and called upon him to lead the people of Israel in an uprising against the Midianites. In true logger fashion, Gideon was at first a little skeptical of the calling. He pointed out to the Lord that he was poor (verse 15), which is the first requirement for being a logger. A logger will always end up poor, so it is best to start out that way or so every logger tells every forester as they sign a cutting contract. Next, like a true logger, Gideon decided to cook a meal. Some of the best steak and fish come from the grill thrown into the back of the boss-logger's pickup truck. But the real logging issue comes in verse twenty-five, when Gideon is given the task of logging a grove. Yes, he is told to go and cut down the images his father was worshipping, and make a fire out of the wood (verses 26 and 27). Gideon takes a young bull (that's his skidder) and goes to cutting.

Perhaps Gideon's daddy summed it up best. When the local folks were in an uproar, he responded with a rather astute observation. One that is so clear that one can only wonder why he fell into worshipping the tree idols in the first place. He says in verse 31b:

"...if he is a god, let him plead for himself, because his altar has been torn down!"

Time to get personal, and don't be surprised, that is why you are reading this. Have any idols in your life? Is there something that towers over you, demanding your worship? Like it or not, you and I are beings who were created to worship, and that is what we will do. We will find something to serve, make no mistake about it. Sex, money, work, status, and fame are always on the top ten lists of modern idols. Leisure activities such as fishing, hunting, and sports are right up there also. We create our own "gods," for the same reason the ancient Midianites and Israelites did. We do not want to be accountable to a righteous God. To do so would require us to ask the inevitable question, "What do you require of me?"

It would be great if we could say "groves" are only found in pagan countries, and that good old church-attending folks are off the hook, but that is not the case. Many a churchgoer has no concept of the God who created this universe we live in. They have cut and pasted their own version, one that will wink at their little sins and not show disapproval of their vices. All they have is a tree, something incapable of thought or communication. A tree is cold and unresponsive to your needs. It cannot give you comfort when you stand at the grave of a friend, nor can it encourage you when you receive that call in the middle of the night. No, a tree can do nothing. Gideon's father had it right. A god incapable of action is no god, and in his case, it was a stump.

Is it time to do a little logging in your life? The process will take hard work, dawn to dusk. Also, be careful of those stumps, they sprout back up. Just when you think you have it under control, you have to cut it again. Keep your ax sharp. Anything that stands between you and God has got to come down. Do not let your job, your bank account, or your hormones dull your saw. Wear your safety equipment and have a first-aid kit nearby. Remember that every day on the logging job has its trials. Your resolve will falter, pressures will mount, and mud will be everywhere; but loggers are tough. Instead of going out on the town, stay at home with the family. Instead of reaching for a "cold one," make a milk-shake with the kids. Turn off the TV and read about Gideon. Find out who this Creator is and about the wonderful life He has for you; and stop hugging the trees!!

Persistence or Longsuffering?

If you are a forester in the Southeastern United States, then you are acquainted with many of the fair woodland creatures that roam the southern woods. If, as a forester, you have land management responsibilities, then you are very acquainted with the subject of this chapter. This little creature doesn't roam the woods, per se; he swims through them. Yes, I am talking about our friend the beaver. Here is a true thorn in the side of woodland owners, unless that woodland owner wants to have his timber die. Beavers have a great history of supplying soft, rich fur for coats and hats. They have a place in history as being the lure to trappers who opened up the West. And they will make your timberland history if you let them. Beavers love a drainage ditch like a kid loves ice cream. Give them a pure, scenic, gently-flowing stream, and in a week, they will turn it into a stagnant pond. Beavers are quietly devastating the Southeast.

There are several reasons for this. One is that they have few predators—no mountain lions, no panthers, and only a few bears. Besides the alligator, few predators want to tackle a full grown—been eating a 120-foot tree from the roots up—beaver. Man can be classified as a predator, but beaver tail soup is not taking the place of the Big Mac any time soon. Fur trappers would starve to death selling the fur, as southern beavers are not as richly adorned as their northern lodge brothers, who have deep, thick fur with a rich texture. Heavy thick coats and hot days don't go together. (See earlier chapter.) Large timberland owners, usually forest industry companies, once had staff foresters or technicians dedicated to trapping beavers to keep them from destroying woodlands; but changes in business practices and downsizing have sent most of these individuals off to pursue other endeavors.

I have learned a lot from beavers over the past years. As a timberland manager, they are a source of constant aggravation; yet at the same time, a source of constant amazement. If you were to take a topographical map of an area with a healthy beaver population, and then give the same map to an engineer and ask him to point to the place on the map where a pond could most easily be started, you would be astounded at the tendency of the two to match. God provided the beaver with a sense of water management and terrain navigation that is at times mind-boggling. But He also gave them some traits that are not so endearing to the woodland's manager; that is, persistence and long-suffering. Now "longsuffering" is a Bible word. You won't find much need for it in your everyday vocabulary. You may mistake it for, or mix it up with "patience," but as I have learned from my furry, web-footed nemeses, there is a dimension to "longsuffering" that is important for us to grasp.

II Peter 3:9 uses "longsuffering" in this way:

The Lord is not slack concerning His promise, as some count slackness, but is longsuffering towards us, not willing that any should perish but that all should come to repentance.

Some of us, probably most of us, are completely lacking in the area of longsuffering. You see, as Peter described it, it is a trait which God has; and we cause Him to use it a lot. It is the idea of patience, hopefulness, and pain all mixed together.

Consider this from the beaver's point of view. You and your family have just completed a treacherous trip up a small stream. You were forced to hit the river by your parents, who decided that the lodge wasn't big enough for all of you. And besides, you were gnawing on all the willow trees, which are your father's favorite food. Having swam and waddled (too many willow tree snacks), you arrive at a beautiful location. There are plenty of trees and a place where the sides of the small valley narrow in towards the stream. It is here you begin building your dam. In an evening, with all the clan working, you have constructed a dam. Water is beginning to pond, and life is good again. After a delicious meal of red maple, you settle in for a nap. Suddenly you are awakened by an alarm. The water level in your lodge is falling. The dam must have broken. As the wife mutters something like, "I told you that right side was too low," you swim to the scene, only to observe the problem is not your construction skills. (Wait until you tell the Mrs.) Rather a local timberland manager with a hoe is raking away your dam.

With a sigh, you wait patiently for him to finish. As the truck drives away, you get to work repairing the dam. By morning, with the repairs completed, you settle in for a good day's sleep. But again, alarms go off, and again you have to go repair the forester's destructive activities. This goes on for days; yet it doesn't really faze you. Yes, it is aggravating at times, but you really want to live here. It is good place. It is worth the bother, and after all, this is what you were made to do. So night after night, you go to work hoping that maybe the forester will give up one day.

Now if I were a beaver, I would be a bit put off after the second attempt, downright insulted after the third, and in a huff to leave after the fourth. "The very idea," I would pout. I would be sure to move away from where I was not wanted.

I wonder if I am that way with people. Have you ever tried to help someone with a problem, only to have them fall again? Perhaps he has a habit that he just can't break or an addiction that controls him. Usually after the second relapse, our response to his cries for help begin to weaken. We get angry with him. We scold him, and too often we just walk away. A beaver is persistent, however. Tear out his dam and he will come back. He is not going to leave until you remove him. He is long-suffering. He will put up with your destructive tendencies because he was made to dam up the stream, and his instincts tell him to do it here.

In a way, that beaver is like his Creator. God loves us. He is not willing that any should perish. We disobey, disappoint, and destroy the very gift of life He gives us. Over and over again, we pull away from His loving embrace, inflicting pain upon the One who loves us. We struggle to get at the very things that will destroy us. While we do this, with a little bit of patience, hopefulness, and a grimace from the pain, He tries again. Often He calls us back to Him with a whisper. Maybe it will be through the words of a friend, perhaps through a doctor. Sometimes it involves a great deal of pain for us, but He is there again, each night, seeking to bring us back to Him, seeking to restore and heal our souls.

Why does He do this? He loves us. It's part of what and who He is. It doesn't make sense to us. Why doesn't He just see that we don't want Him in our lives and leave us alone? Thankfully, He doesn't listen to our denials of needing Him, but rather He listens to our hearts. The heart He created within us desires a relationship with the Creator. We cry out for healing, for the broken places to be made whole, to have the gaping holes in our lives filled and purpose restored.

Think about that the next time you don the hip waders to go rake out a beaver dam. Think about a Heavenly Father who is not willing to let you go, not willing to let you become a shattered, useless creation. He has a plan and purpose for you, and He will be long-suffering with you. Will you surrender your rake?

Dams and Damnation

In the fifteenth verse of the opening chapter of his epistle, James, the brother of Christ, exhorts his readers of the subtleness of sin. It begins with a look, a lust, then turns into sin, and then comes tragic death. Sin usually doesn't hit you upside the head, and drag you away; rather it comes slowly, gently tugging at you, until you are surrounded in a quagmire of death. His warning is found in chapter 1, verse 15, of the book by his name:

Then, when desire (lust) has conceived, it gives birth to sin; and sin, when it is full-grown, brings forth death.

The act of being punished for your sins, of being sent to eternal torment, is called "damnation." Not a very pleasant thought, and certainly not to be taken as lightly as the word is nowadays. Put the dictionary back on the shelf, and let's take a hike.

It was a nice, quiet little piece of woods when we first found it, with strong, healthy trees, and gentle, rolling hills of a southern variety. For those of you from the mountains, gently-rolling hills mean you don't have to break a sweat or catch your breath when you walk up it. There in the middle was a nice stream flowing on towards some distant river. A picture of Psalm 1 comes to mind, where David talks about trees being planted by the rivers of water, bringing forth fruit.

That is often the purpose of water—bringing life. Take a stroll across the prairie or across a desert and you can find water by looking for trees. That is the only place that life seems to flourish, at the water's edge. Here in our little dale, it is no different. The soil is well-drained by the stream, keeping the water level low, and constant. Heavy rains will quickly run off, and dry periods will still find moisture under the stream bed. All is as it should be.

From our vantage point on the side of the dale, halfway up the rolling hillside, we couldn't quite make out the critter. It was moving up stream, waddling a little as it went, occasionally finding a spot deep enough to swim. It was kind of cute, just a ball of fur. And, say, look at that flat tail. Yes, it's a beaver! It doesn't make much of a disturbance, even though it seems to have found a spot of interest. There where that small tributary comes in, the beaver appears to be mudding up the water somewhat. But it is soon gone, and the stream will clear, and it is getting late.

Upon our next visit to the dale, we find that our furry friend has been busy. At the stream junction, we can see numerous sticks and debris accumulated. We notice the flow of the water has slowed a little, but it is still flowing. Aren't beavers industrious?!

Each visit shows the rapid and steady construction of the dam. Water starts to back up as its forward progress is impeded. Small trees along the stream's bank have been cut down, and spike-like stumps salute the newly constructed dam. With some alarm now, we realize that this is not good for our little valley. We need water flowing, so in haste we tear at the dam, relieved to see and hear the water rushing back on its path to the distant river. But with every return, we find that the beaver has rebuilt. His dam is growing in size as the water backs-up behind it. What was once a five foot stream is now one hundred feet across, and the small little dam resembles something named after President Hoover. We shrug our shoulders, and resign ourselves to the fact that it is just natural. That is the way things go.

Time passes. When next we return, we stand gazing in dismay. Our little dale is a graveyard of dead trees. The water that once nourished them has now drowned them. No beautiful leaves here, just limbless trunks. Stark tree skeletons scream at the sky. Their silent accusations hang in the air. Long past, has been any chance to rescue or save. No life lines can be thrown to these poor ghosts of trees past. Sediment, carried by the stream, now is daily deposited in the pond. It can no longer be carried along on the current of the once free-flowing stream. The sediment sinks, clinging to everything, coating all with a layer of slime and mud. Where once the earth was firm and animals walked with regularity, now layers of mud suck on all who venture to enter. The odor of death permeates the air: decaying trees and plants, rotting leaves, stagnant water.

If only we could have kept out that beaver. It was so cute. We liked to watch it, but we never planned on the mess it had made; we never planned on the loss and destruction of the land and timber we so enjoyed. That dam brought death. It changed everything—the hydrology, the herbaceous cover, the animal life, and the insect population.

Imagine the Garden of Eden. (What a picture!) It is the perfect garden, with good fruit, and Adam had the perfect job of looking after it. There he once walked and talked with God, but sin came in and with it death. Sin looks so innocent at first. We watch it awhile, attracted to the possibilities, but then it starts to take hold. Soon it has a foundation we can't shake. We realize our error and scramble to correct it, but often it is too late, or we don't really try all that hard.

Sin is the dam that stops the life-giving flow. Jesus spoke of a water that gave life, he called it Living Water, the water that will bring life to our dying souls.

John 4:14 says:

"...but whoever drinks of the water that I shall give him will never thirst. But the water that I shall give him will become in him a fountain of water springing up into everlasting life."

Is there a dam in your life, something that is keeping that water from reaching you, from bringing life to you? Just as sure as a beaver pond will flood and kill vast acreages of timber, sin will kill you. Only Christ can remove the dam, only the blood of Jesus can restore the stream of life into your soul. Dams and damnation both bring death, but both can be conquered.

Culverts

Certainly, this is a topic that is near the forefront of every seminary's curriculum. What is a culvert, and how can it be used to further God's Kingdom? Of course, we all know what a culvert is, and have driven over them daily for as long as we have been riding in the horseless carriage. The culvert is simply a pipe placed under a road; or in one old woods path I found, a hollow cypress log. For an example of your own, try looking at your driveway the next time you are outside. Usually there will be a culvert at the roadside ditch. That culvert allows water to pass under your driveway instead of over it. Remember that definition, it might show up on a test at the end of the book.

When it comes time to access a block of timber, either for logging it or for the sake of managing it, the first step is laying out a road. How else are we going to get there? As we lay out our proposed road, often we find that there are one or more streams or ditches that must be crossed if we are to get from Point A to Point B.

If you want to break any drought, follow these steps. The forester looks at the tract of timber and decides he can lay out a temporary road. He ignores the need for a culvert because the summer has been dry and there is no water in the stream. He has the logger move in, and cutting begins. After the first few days, the logger has valuable timber cut and lying on the ground, waiting to be loaded. It is then, that in nine out of ten cases, the drought will break. Rain, unseen since the days of Noah, will descend from the clouds. The dry, little stream is now rejoicing in renewal. And as it rejoices, it grows in volume, rising against the side of the road, until it reaches the surface of the road, and begins to once again carve out its original channel. When the forester returns days later, he usually finds that the little access road is no more. For the lack of a culvert, the stream has destroyed his road. Now he must start over, regroup, and spend more money. All the time, the "money clock" is ticking. The logger can't get to his equipment; he can't make loads; which means he can't make his payments, and the mill can't get wood--all because of the lack of a culvert.

Culverts allow water to go about its business, flowing along happily; and the road above can do its job, which is to provide a foundation for transportation. Without a reliable culvert, water flow can be blocked until it reaches critical mass, and it will then seek some means to follow gravity. Watch any news report of major floods, and you will see that when water decides to follow gravity, not much will stand in its path.

Let's keep the culverts. Let's make sure they are large enough to handle the expected water flow, and let's keep them from being clogged. I had a tract with a cantankerous culvert. It always seemed to find logs, sticks, mud, and leaves and anything else lying around; and it would somehow stuff itself with these items to the point that no water could pass through it. I soon found out that the culvert was having help, and the helpers belonged to a rowdy, local beaver colony. It seemed to be their favorite pastime. They would hide quietly while I raked out the debris; and with disdain they would watch my satisfied smile as the water again flushed under the road instead of over it. They would stay hidden even while I would call for more rocks and sand to be delivered to make the road drivable again. Then that night, they would get their gang together and stuff every log and limb they could find into the mouth of that culvert; laughing hysterically no doubt, as the water quickly rose up and washed away my road. To be true culverts, water had to pass through them, and this group was making sure I had no culverts.

Culverts and what they are used for, can give us a picture of prayer. How are we supposed to pray? Christ gave instructions to His disciples concerning prayer, of how to talk to God, to communicate with Him. In Matthew 6:9-13, Jesus offers us an example of prayer. Look closely at verse 12:

"And forgive us our debts, as we forgive our debtors."

Now that's pretty basic. It's a plea for forgiveness. How often do we pray that portion of verse 12, *"forgive us our debts"?* But seldom do we pray the rest of the verse, the part about us forgiving someone else. Jesus goes further in verse 14, and what He says is very sobering. If we do not forgive others, then God cannot forgive us. Let that sink in for a minute. Ever hold a grudge? Ever refuse to talk to someone because they offended you in some way?

Life, events, and circumstances all keep coming at us. Many things are out of our control. We cannot control how others may act, but we can control our response. And the Bible tells us we have to forgive if we want God's forgiveness. When someone does us wrong, we have to forgive them whether—sit down for this—they say they are sorry or not. You see, it's like a culvert. We have to let those instances of hurt and anger flow on past. We cannot allow them to build up against us and inside us until they reach a critical mass and then explode. Explosions are not good. Valuable time and effort is wasted, progress is set back, often abandoned all together.

Forgiveness: it is an open culvert, allowing those instances of hurt and anger to flow on past us. Let them go. Why destroy the road? Have you ever heard the saying, "Don't burn your bridges"? Bridges make it possible to use the road, for you and for others. My adaptation of that saying is: "Use the right culvert, and keep it open." Perhaps the best example of showing forgiveness would be Jesus Himself. While hanging on a cross, beaten, dying, and suffering for my sins and yours, He looked at those people, the very people who were cursing and taunting Him, and forgave them (Luke 23:34). What an example! What a challenge! Keeping the culvert open will often be a chore. Emotions will seek to clog it. Anger will push mud into it. But keep working at it. Take the rake out yet again, and forgive. Let the water flow. Save the road for you and others.

Follow the River

I am a professional woodsman. I make my living outdoors. I have degrees and certificates that credit me with professional status. I have twenty-twenty vision. I am not color blind. I have a compass. All of these thoughts, as they related to my competence, raced through my mind one morning as I debated whether I was lost, or simply misplaced. You see, it started so innocently. I was marking a tract of timber for a veneer customer; that is to say, I was spray-painting trees. The trees met the criteria needed for customers who peel logs to make paneling. These logs are valuable, and it often pays to mark them ahead of time, to keep them from getting placed in the wrong pile at the log deck. The sale area, some forty acres, was part of a larger 179-acre tract I was managing. It was bordered by a field on one side, a river on the other, and similar woods on the other two sides. Yet here I was, without a clue as to where I was, and worse yet, where my truck was.

Here is the skinny on what happened. I ran out of paint, the last can I had. This meant it was time to return to the truck, and then to the next item on my agenda for that day. I took a compass reading toward the field, checked the shadows from the trees, and started my ten minute stroll. It was a beautiful fall day, sunny and cool. Need I say more? In the course of my walk, I came upon a flagged sale line, representing the sides of the sale area I had flagged earlier in the day. Figuring this to be the south line, and knowing my truck lay to the "right" of this line, I continued my walk, thinking about where to pick up some lunch. After about twenty minutes, I realized that something was amiss. My first clue was the river. There it was, big, wide, and right in my path. But my path was not supposed to be anywhere in the vicinity of the river. I consulted my compass again, only to find that the bearing did indeed continue across the river.

Here I began scratching my head. The distant flagged line I had crossed now came to mind, and the thought that perhaps it was the north line I had crossed, and not the south line, which meant that I had walked off the property for some distance. Without a map or a clear idea of where I was, I decided to go by the tried and true method of wilderness survival— "Follow the River." You see, the river flowed south, and going south would cause me to cross at least three lines, two flagged, and one painted. Each of them would place me back on the property, and from there I could easily follow a line back to my truck. It was just a matter of walking, and I am a professional. Besides, it was a nice day for a stroll along a flowing river.

A nice buck deer jumped into the water and swam for the safety of the other side. While watching it, I decided to drop down along the grassy river bank to find easier walking. Coming to a bend in the river, I climbed the bank and found a nice deer trail and a very impressive antler rub on a cedar tree. I walked on. After measuring a mile, I realized that something was not right. There was no way I could have traveled more than a mile and not crossed one of the three lines, unless I had simply missed them and walked right past. I backtracked for a half mile, but still there were no lines in sight. At that point, my ten minute stroll had lasted an hour.

With resignation to many of the aforementioned thoughts, including some on my sanity, I resigned myself to follow the river all the way downstream to a road bridge and then hike back several miles to my truck from the bridge. This was not on my agenda. An hour later, I was still walking. Something was not right. The bridge was not that far. I sat down and took a break, prayed, and drew a map in the dirt.

Then it was off down the river. I took a trail along a grassy shore line, and then climbed up the bank at a trail, noticing a nice deer rub on a cedar tree. There was no time to study it. It did bring to mind an earlier rub, though. I wondered—no, I was following a river, and rivers do not do loops. I thought, "*I cannot be going in circles.*" Just past the rub I found a nice antler shed, half of an eight pointer. It was from last year, and probably the same deer who was working over all the cedar trees he could find along the bank. Normally I would carry it out with me, but not today.

Thirty minutes later, as I cut across a grassy riverbank and up the bank at the side, where an old deer trail led past a...rubbed...cedar tree!

I then realized that somehow, I had been walking in circles, or that the river was not a river, or that I was flipping out. I took out my knife and marked the cedar tree. Walking on *downstream*, I saw a little holly tree. As I suspected, under its branches lay an antler shed, four points out of eight. As I accepted the fact of having walked for hours in circles, I struck out in new resolve, this time keeping to the bank, no matter how tough the briars or brush would become; and no shortcuts!

I could then see it. As I walked that stretch, I could see through the woods, and there the river lay. The river on my left, a twisting little thing, no doubt curved just ahead, and by cutting through the woods, I saved some walking. Once I hit the river again, I followed it downstream. Only what I was seeing, was where I had been.

Later, when I arrived at the office, I looked at a photo of the area, and sure enough, the river made a sharp double loop, nearly touching itself—the ingredients for a future oxbow lake. Once I solved the loop, I returned and found my flagged line, a mere five minutes away, and ten minutes later, I was back in the front seat of my Blazer. The loop was nearly a mile in length, and I had been stuck in it for at least three laps.

While praying a prayer of thanks, I was reminded of John 5. Jesus is at Bethesda. Scriptures states there was a multitude of sick folks lying under the porch, waiting for a chance to move into the pool for healing. There was a multitude. The same word was used when great throngs would follow Jesus to hear Him preach. And here Jesus is, alone, walking through, around, and among the sick folks. He stops. Verse 6 records His question to one who is lying, alone, crippled, sick:

"...Do you want to be made well?"

This can be translated as "Do you want to get better?" This would be an obvious question to one who is unable to do anything about it. Then Christ gives him a simple solution, recorded in verse 8:

"Rise, take up your bed and walk."

Now, looking further into the chapter, we find in verse 13 that the man had no idea who Jesus was. So a stranger, tells him to stand up and walk, and he does. What made him try it? Thirty-eight years of lying on his back, and now someone says do this simple thing, arise and walk. And yet there was something in his voice. He did not seem to be making a suggestion, rather he meant for him to stand and walk. The request was rather simple. Had the stranger promised healing in exchange for deeds of kindness or money? The man no doubt would have done all he could have done to make the grade. After all, he had lain there under the porch for such a promise, a promise that only said, "When the angel stirs the water, get into the water first!" (See verse 4.)

My situation at the river boiled down to simplicity. Regardless of my training, I was lost. Regardless of my intentions, I was lost. I was stuck in a loop that made no sense, looking for a way out and trying shortcuts. Are you caught in a loop of destruction and hopelessness?

Seems like you have been here before doesn't it? When will you decide that you are ready to be found? When will the hard floor of desperation cause you to look for the One who can supply the answer? There He is, walking among us, moving from one sick soul to another, not forcing Himself on anyone. He is just asking a simple question, "Do you want to be saved?" We would be fools to say, "No." No one wants to be lost or to be stuck in a hopeless loop for eternity without help or hope. "Yes," is the reply we must give, or we risk His passing by.

His prescription is simple, and he records it in Romans 10:9

...that if you confess with your mouth the Lord Jesus and believe in your heart that God has raised Him from the dead, you will be saved.

In other words, stop relying on your training, on your instincts, on taking shortcuts, or on your sense of direction. It is so simple— "Follow the River."

And he showed me a pure river of water of life, clear as crystal, proceeding from the throne of God and of the Lamb.

Revelation 22:1

Stump Holes

It took me a while to really understand the "what" and the "why," but eventually I have come to understand the greatly misunderstood stump hole. Unfortunately, neither I nor anyone else can fully grasp the "where." Stump holes are based on a few very important facts. You could call them the fundamental elements in the world of stump holes. Just as you have hydrogen and oxygen combining to form water, so do leaves and decay combine to form the dreaded stump hole. Now stump holes have often been given a lot more credit than they deserve. While it has never been actually captured on film, they are reported to be very mobile and have the capacity to move from spot to spot, hiding themselves with leaves, lying in wait for the unsuspecting forester to walk by. For those who prefer concrete under your feet, let me stop and explain the stump hole.

Two things must be understood before we go any further. They are critical to understanding the world of the stump holes. They are: wood decays; and leaves, by and of themselves, cannot hold up the weight of a full-grown man. It begins when a tree ends, and particularly with the end still in the ground. A tree is harvested or is blown over, and the roots and a portion of the trunk are all that remain. This trunk portion may or may not stick out of the ground; it really doesn't matter—yet. First you need decay. With the help of the aforementioned hydrogen and oxygen, and lots of bugs, mold, fungus, etc., the stump begins to dissolve. As it does, the local leaf population lying on the forest floor, still upset with being castaway the fall before, devises an insidious revenge on all who pass by. They target all who had absently trampled upon them, treating them like so much discarded carpet. Yes, they will have their revenge. They begin by covering the stump, hiding it, building a roof of leaves over it, creating an even better environment for the work of the decay, and more to the point, hiding the very location of the stump.

Time passes. More leaves fall. Decay has eaten away the once solid stump. As it decays, thanks to the leaf canopy, there is now a nice vacant hole, as if the stump had been physically dug out of the ground and a nice bed sheet was spread across the top of the hole. Now you have a stump hole. It is a hole in the ground, as large as the original tree. It is deeper than any boots you may or may not be wearing, and completely covered by a layer of leaves, slyly woven together to form a clever carpet that hides the stump hole from all.

Perhaps you have seen or read about tiger traps. To make one a large pit is dug, sharpened stakes are placed in the bottom of the pit, and then a straw mat is placed over the top. Along comes a tiger, which steps on the mat, falls into the pit, and is pierced by the stakes in the bottom. The locals celebrate with a tiger roast. Stump holes are the same thing, and often they include shards of decaying wood sticking up like sharpened stakes at the bottom! As the forester walks over the leaf mat, the ground gives way, and—whoosh! —he falls straight down with one leg, jarred to a stop either by the bottom of the hole, or by the snapping of his other leg as it hits the ground.

Stump holes are the homes of many creatures that do not like the sudden intrusion. I have pulled my leg out of these holes to find snakes, bees, and bugs which I wanted no part of, following my foot out, looking to have a conversation with the owner of said boot; and seeking reparations and repairs to their domicile. I regret to say that I have never stayed to have the pleasure of talking with any of them.

The worst stump holes are the ones in water. They not only hide under a canopy of leaves, but also silt. The best way to find these monsters is to send the young technician working with you across the swamp first. It helps if he has boots on, but that truthfully doesn't matter. (Water in a stump hole is always one inch higher than your boots.) Try to get your laughter out of the way while he is flailing in the water trying to get out. That way he won't get mad.

Stump holes are hidden, waiting silently for you to step upon them, unaware, unprepared. Then down you go. Water fills your boot. There is a jarring pain in your knee, and whatever you had in your hand is thrown out in front of you in surprise. At best you have a wet foot. At worst, your knee or ankle is broken, or the occupant of the hole puts a "hurtin" on you. Regardless, way back in the woods, stump holes are problems.

Consider Job, and his story, which begins in Job 1, paraphrased as follows:

> "Master Job, the Sabeans have raided the pastures, killed the servants and carried away all the livestock!"

> "Master Job, fire from heaven killed the servants and the sheep!"

> "Master Job, the Chaldeans have killed the servants and they have carried away the camels!"

> "Master Job, a great wind has destroyed and taken the lives of your children!"

Stump holes in life, they are sudden surprises that come with no warning. They jar us. They surprise us. They hurt us. The phone rings in the night, and our lives forever change. The report is back from the doctor— "just routine," they said. They will call you with the results, but now it demands an appointment. You thought it couldn't happen, or that no one would know. Now it has, and now they do. We were just minding our own business, walking through the woods, doing our job, whistling a tune. Now it has changed.

Stump holes weren't listed as being created during that first week of creation when trees were, but they were foreshadowed. There was one in the Garden. Right there by that good looking fruit tree. You see, not all stump holes are well hidden. By that I mean, there are ways to look for them. Some we can find by observation, or by examination. The realization that they are present will help us find them. You can bet they are in a stagnant swamp, so use a pole to probe ahead as you walk. If you are on an old pine ridge, watch out. Stump holes are real, and they do exist.

Here's some advice for those walking through the terrain of life:

BIBLES, BEAVERS, AND BIG TIMBER

Proverbs 1:7-12,15 *The fear of the Lord is the beginning of knowledge, but fools despise wisdom and instruction. My son, hear the instruction of your father, and do not forsake the law of your mother; for they will be a graceful ornament on your head, and chains about your neck. My son, if sinners entice you, do not consent. If they say, "Come with us, let us lie in wait to shed blood; let us lurk secretly for the innocent without cause; let us swallow them alive like Sheol* (grave), *and whole, like those that go down to the Pit...My son, do not walk in the way with them, keep your foot from their path...*

But what of those holes we can't see, the ones like Job crashed into? He wasn't living in sin, or running with the wrong crowd. According to Chapter 1 of Job, he was the best Christian on the planet. If he couldn't see the holes, how can we?

God made the stump hole, as much as I hate to admit it. It was His tree, His roots. The leaves that fell and covered the hole were of His design. The decay and insect life that contributed to the vacating of the stump were set in motion by His Word. And if you have ever walked through the woods, no matter how hard you try not to, you will step into a stump hole. Sometimes it will be because we failed to stay on the path. The stump holes are there to reprove us, to punish us for our wandering from God's path. Sometimes it is because we have to travel through the woods. I have noticed that everyone I know, regardless of their relationship with God, will get sick, and they all eventually will die. No one is immune to these stump holes. They are a part of our lives.

If we are walking in the woods, there MUST BE dead trees, former trees, trees that have fallen and decayed, leaving a hole in the ground; and if we are in the world, there must be sickness, and distress, and death, because we live in a fallen world. Since Eve and Adam slammed to the bottom of that first stump hole, our lives must also be filled with them. Some are punishing, others are just a part of life. We must have faith in a sovereign God. The same God who created the trees, created the stump holes. Allow Him to use them in your life, to use them for reproof if needed, or to draw you closer to Him.

Job, after dragging himself from the stump holes, is quoted as saying:

Job 13:15a *"Though he slay me, yet will I trust Him..."*

To trust the Lord, the creator of the stump hole, is to trust that the Creator has placed the hole according to His plan and His purpose, and that our tears, our fears, are not without notice, and not without the compassion of our God. As David put it:

Psalms 139:7 *Where can I go from Your Spirit? Or where can I flee from Your presence?*

It's good to know someone is in the woods with you to help you out of the stump hole.

Road Building 101

"Nice wood, but how are you going to get it out?" Such is the question asked daily if you happen to work in the southeastern Coastal Plain. A sudden change in elevation, even a foot or so, can cause a drastic change in the composition of your forest. Out of a stagnant, hardwood swamp, rises an island, an island of loblolly pine, with age and size, and a market value that would stagger the mind. I am thinking of one such island in particular. Years of advancing, aggressive beaver activity had turned a lowland hardwood area into one-hundred acres of soaking wet natural disaster area. Silt and sediment from floods, captured by the dams, spread out over the area, had created a real boot-sucking swamp. The kind of place that just to travel two-hundred yards on foot was next to impossible. Trees, dead from too much water or from having their bark removed by the local "flat-tail" population, lay scattered through the water, hidden from view by mud, grass, and hordes of mosquitoes.

But I had seen a vision. No, it wasn't induced by heat, humidity, and mosquitoes; though I have had a few of those too. Actually it really wasn't much of a vision. It was more like a photograph. The local USDA office, a good place for photographs of the local topography, carried photographs of the aforementioned swamp. There in the swamp they stood—pine trees. Now pine trees don't grow in swamps as a rule, so if you see them on a photograph you can bet there is something dry underneath them. With this information in hand, the quest began to reach the island. I tried from several directions, always reaching some uncrossable stretch of swamp where the water depth was too great, or the distance and my aching knees said it was time to turn back.

Finally I devised a plan, and that plan called for water reduction. The local wood-chewer's union did not appreciate my plan, especially when several of them were forced to vacate the premises. But over a few months, I was able to drop the level of the water to the point where I could make it across to the island—and what an island!

Now a good stand of mature southern pine might sell for as much as $4,000 per acre in a strong market, but this island made a new definition of "good." It was old, having seen many winters, actually close to eighty of them. It stood over 120 feet tall, and priced out at over $8,000 per acre. It was stunning.

"Nice wood, but how are you going to get it out?"

It is important to remember that a log truck, fully loaded with logs, weighs in at 90,000 pounds. It is also important to remember, fully loaded log trucks do not float. If the island could not be brought to the road, then the road would have to be brought to the island. Thus began the road building. First we had to control the water. That meant an agreement had to be reached with the local wood-chewer's union. Upon reaching an agreement, we began laying out the road. To do this we had to find a hill, a hill that would allow us to stay above the water, to build up a road. Now as I previously stated, this area was under water. So we had to look elsewhere for the hill. We found it, just a quarter mile away, a nice hill of sand. From it, we began to make a foundation. (And yes, we had permits.) The foundation was brought in via dump trucks and excavators, and we began to fashion a road. Moving the hill from where it was to where we needed our road, we created a sandy path along our route. Which over several days began to harden into a road bed. Culverts were placed to allow water to pass under the road, and suddenly, the hill had provided us with an elevated road. The valuable timber could be hauled, and the question could be answered:

"We're going to haul it right out this road."

The angels, shaking their heads, might have asked God one day: "See anything of value out there?"

They could see that the world was a big mess.

Romans 3:12b-17 *"...There is none who does good, no, not one. Their throat is an open tomb; with their tongues they have practiced deceit; the poison of asps is under their lips; whose mouth is full of cursing and bitterness. Their feet are swift to shed blood; destruction and misery are in their ways; and the way of peace they have not known."*

What could a holy God see in such a mess? What would cause Him to love a bunch of degenerates like man? Selfish, arrogant creatures we are, and yet God looked at His world...and looked at the people...and saw value in them.

John 3:16a *"For God so loved the world..."*

"Okay, you love them, but how are you going to get them out?"

Romans 5:8-10 *But God demonstrates His own love towards us, in that while we were still sinners, Christ died for us. Much more then, having now been justified by His blood, we shall be saved from wrath through Him. For if when we were enemies we were reconciled to God through the death of His Son, much more, having been reconciled, we shall be saved by His life.*

God looked at where we were, and where He was, and decided to make a path. He looked at the swamp of sin we live in, the death and decay, and knew he needed to create a way to get us out. As He looked around, He saw a hill. Luke 23:33 gives it a name; Calvary. It was a simple hill, but one that would provide the foundation for a road. A path would be made. We would be given a means of escape.

"...that whoever believes in Him should not perish but have everlasting life." (John 3:16)

It doesn't say it is automatic. It doesn't give blanket coverage to everyone. It says to those who believe in Jesus, a way of escape has been given; eternal life is available.

We stand in the swamp faced with a question. Around us is death and decay. We can't swim it, or walk it. It is too large for the best and biggest of us. "How are we going to get out?"

A hill was found; a road was established. We have to decide if we will use it to escape the swamp.

Logging and Lepers

If you have read the chapters of this book in order so far, then you are familiar with the species known as "Surprisamis maximus," or locally referred to as the "stump hole." I had the early morning pleasure of meeting one of the more advanced of the species a few days ago. It happened on a logging job. The logger was working on a very wet piece of ground. By wet, I mean the water was measurable in terms of feet. Now, what allowed the logger to work was a vast array of mortgages, all of which were attached to high-tech logging equipment. There were three machines that had metal tracks like a tank would have, moving across the mud and through the timber without any problems. These machines had the capacity to cut and grab entire trees, lifting them into the air, and setting them down into neat piles. After the trees were cut and piled, along came another set of machines, these had rubber tires, and lots of them. One, called a clam-bunk skidder, had sixteen wheels in all. Another machine, called a skidder, had tires four feet wide. As a group, they could virtually go anywhere, as long as the water was not over the motors of the equipment. Now since this logger was working, that meant that I had to work. In particular, logging operations require on-the-ground inspections, to ensure that trees are being picked up, cut properly, and boundary lines are being observed.

When I was a youngster, folks would always point at my feet, and say such things like, "He's going to be tall" or "That boy has a firm foundation," to which my parents would mumble something about the soaring cost of shoes. Needless to say, I have big feet, size 13. (Now I am good enough in math to know that 13 inches is a lot smaller than 4 feet; and having 2 legs is not like having 16; and even a big shoe is not spread wide like a metal track.) Thus, I do not maneuver in wet terrain with near the agility that this special equipment can. But follow it I must. Trying to walk on branches and pieces of logs, I gingerly make my way to the far boundary. If a machine can make it, then so can a nimble-footed forester. It is here that the *Surprisamis maximus* made its surprise entry.

Now before we continue, let's discuss water turbidity. Don't have a clue do you? Missed that day in biology didn't you. Okay, let's talk about muddy water. Trees grow in dirt. Dirt plus water equals mud. If you take logging equipment, add two feet of standing water, you will get muddy water. The more the equipment passes through the water, the more mud. Got the picture? Now back to the stump hole. I never saw it coming. I was traversing across the top of a limb, and stepping into water that just a second ago was barely below my boot tops. (I should have been listening for the change in the theater music; I should have noticed all the woodland creatures pausing to watch my next step, but no, I plunged ahead...literally.) Plunge; just saying the word makes me look for a towel. The only thing that kept me from doing a full Jacque Cousteau was the grabbing of a tree stump as I passed by. There I was, neck deep in muddy water, three hours from home, nine-thirty in the morning; and it was the middle of January. If I had wanted to go swimming, I could have walked to the lake near my house, where at least the water was clean, though probably just as cold.

The experience reminded me of the story of Naaman, found in II Kings 5. Naaman was in charge of the army of Syria, the general as we would know him. He was also a leper. Leprosy was the kiss of death. Working away on the skin, it soon made the bearer an outcast, and then it made them a corpse. Now as part of a recent war against Israel, Naaman had taken captive a young girl to be his servant. This young girl, while being a prisoner of war, still had the foundation of a solid upbringing. She had learned the lessons of Sunday school quite well. She took the initiative and went to Naaman's wife and told her about Elisha, the mighty prophet in her hometown, who served the true and living God. Elisha, she said, could cure her master. Naturally, the wife tells the wonderful news to Naaman, who talks to the king. The king tells Naaman to get an entourage together. With his party assembled, he heads off to be healed. The cure awaits him in Samaria. Now upon arriving, Naaman expected some grand ceremony befitting the occasion: horns, trumpets, dancers, the works. It would be something tasteful, slightly extravagant, not as much for a king, but fitting for a general. After all, the last time he was here he "spanked" the local militia. What he got instead, was a second party message delivered by a servant, to go dip in the muddy Jordan River seven times.

He was not a happy camper. Forget the poor delivery of the message; forget the complete lack of fanfare and applause. And certainly they could forget anything that had to do with the muddy Jordan River. "Why the rivers of my hometown are clean, why not use them!" he thundered. In his aggravation and in a huff, he was ready to leave—split, adios, hit the road. But he still had the plague. The death sentence was still hanging over him. His good faith in coming, all his efforts to find and arrive at Elisha's door had not cured him, nor had it reduced the grip that the vile disease.

Thankfully, his servants were also his friends, and they continued to urge him to obey the prescription that was delivered; and willing to try anything to survive the plague that was leprosy, he stepped into the water. Now his faith level can't be too high at this point. I can see him pause with each dip.

"Seven times, are you sure?"

"Look at this mud, I will be a mess."

"What if it stirs up my leprosy?"

He begins the dipping, and after six times, nothing is happening, and his rage is surely building, but hope is also fleeting. Dripping with muddy water, he plunges in one more time. I wonder if he felt it first while under the water: the skin tingling, tightening, and healing, sores disappearing? In verse 14, it refers to his flesh as childlike, soft and clean.

What a ludicrous way to get cured. It was so simple. So simple that Naaman nearly refused to do it. Imagine, being healed by muddy water. Yet, Jesus offers us the same simple cure. We suffer from spiritual leprosy, it's called sin; and it's a disease that is making us an outcast from God the Father, causing us to become a corpse, to be separated for all eternity from the presence of God.

Hebrews 7:25 *Therefore He is also able to save to the uttermost those who come to God through Him, since He always lives to make intercession for them.*

Jesus said in John 14:6 that we need only come to him: *"I am the way, the truth, and the life. No one comes to the Father except through Me."*

To believe that Jesus is the Son of God, that He died for my sins, and that He rose from the grave sounds pretty thin. That's no way to cure us from eternal death. How about something grander, something we can participate in? It may be climbing a great mountain, or swimming a sea. How about working at a local mission or doing time in the church nursery?

Naaman began with great skepticism. But given the choice between leprosy and death, or doing something as simple as dipping seven times in a river, he placed what little bit of faith he had in the words of Elisha. Elisha was a man he had not seen, nor met up to this point; but under he went. But as he came out the seventh time, his faith was no longer little or weak. He had been healed. Here we are, dying from sin, no way to get healed, except to accept Christ's free gift. Opening that gift will change your life. It gets your attention, like stepping into a stump hole full of cold, muddy water!

Knots

I had the chance to tour the Mariner's Museum, in Newport News, Virginia today. It was an interesting way for a forester to spend his day. Not many trees to see in the ocean. I did enjoy the hands-on areas. In one section, they had an area to practice your knot tying. You know the classic bowline knot we all learn as kids, but never recognize the use for it. In this same area however, were several boats and canoes, and all were made of wood. Now when I see wood, I light up. The carpenter and the forester in me wants to know about the wood, and about the tools used to put it all together. What folks could do before electric tools were available is amazing. Here however, of more interest was the kind of wood they used. It was knot-free wood. As I looked from stern to bow on these beautifully crafted boats, there were no knots to be seen. The only knots on a wooden boat are the ones in the ropes. You see, knots leak. Knots also weaken the wood, and knots are unsightly. "No knots," seems to be the cry of the wooden boat builders. And it was not just an American thing. They had boats from all over the world, and they all were free from the dreaded scourge of the knot.

To the inquiring mind comes the question; where do knots come from and who needs them? In traversing the forests of this great land, one will find a singular common thread among all trees—they have branches. Some branches may be as big as the tree itself, others may be nothing short of whips, but if it is a tree it has branches. Branches are important to a tree. You could almost say it gives a tree its distinct character. If you pick up any good dendrology book—that's tree identification to you laymen—you will see along with the descriptions of the leaves and fruit, a silhouette of the tree in its natural, free-growing state. The way the branches come off the main tree trunk or bole, is very distinctive to various tree species. Some branches come out at right angles, others with a slant upwards or down. Many come out, up, and then curve down. Some change as the branches progress up the stem.

Given this fact, that all trees have branches of some sort, and branches cause knots, then where does knot-free lumber come from? The mill manager from your company's sawmill will say it comes from your main competitor's sawmill. The best logs always show up down the road at someone else's saw mill. While your mill has a yard full of expensive, knotty logs, the mill down the road has a fine collection of large, knot-free logs, and loggers trying to donate more. The mill manager swears the other mill is making money on the clear wood that they have in inventory, while your logs are being rejected by the local cement contractors. Before the mill managers and the procurement foresters come to blows, let's get into the woods and look at how knots are generally formed.

First consider that a young growing sapling must have as much leaf coverage as possible, thus allowing it to capture sunlight and produce the ingredients needed for its survival. To accomplish this, it begins to sprout branches as soon as it clears the surface of the ground. Now as it grows, more of the leaf mass begins to be supported by the upper branches, causing a nice cool shade to fall on the lower branches. Shade, often sought by many a hot forester, affects foresters and branches the same. Work comes to a halt. Without the sunlight, the leaves supported by the branches will begin to drop off, and soon the branch will find it no longer has a reason to be. In theory, the branch will then drop from the bole, and the growing tree will begin to "scab" over the spot where the branch once was attached to the trunk. The longer the tree has to put fresh new wood tissue over this spot, the clearer (knot free) the wood becomes. Obviously, the sooner a tree discards its lower branches, the sooner it can begin to put down clear wood. The trouble begins when the branches are not discarded like they should be. Talk to anyone in the southern pine growing business, and they will tell you that getting a tree to shed its lower branches in a timely fashion is never guaranteed. It would seem some trees just want to hold on to those branches; that they want knots!

The next step taken by the timber grower is to try to convince the consumer that they want to buy wood with knots. It gives the wood character. I would tend to agree with them as I enjoy a good yellow pine wall as well as anyone. Just come to my house. Yellow pine walls, floors, and cabinets will greet you. But don't give me a boat made of yellow pine. Not without a bailing can and a life jacket. Character is okay, but not when it interferes with the purpose of the wood.

We all have "knots" in our lives, branches of character. Some are good. They help to define who we are. Old Uncle Dexter, what a character! He ate coffee beans and drank Yoo-Hoos every day of his life until he was run-over by a produce truck while riding his bicycle up Hickory Mountain to attend his eightieth birthday party! When we talk about character, often it is those things, those "knots" that cause us to stand out as individuals.

But there are also bad knots. They cause our ship to leak, and the walls of our boat to become weak. The beauty of our vessel is marred and disfigured. Bad knots are habits or tendencies that we carry with us, and refuse to drop. Instead of pruning or reducing the energy to feed them, we keep pumping "sunlight" to them, allowing the branch to flourish, allowing the delay of better wood to be produced. The excuses are often the same: "It's just who I am," or "That's the way God made me," or "I've been this way so long there's no way to change now." It is sad to harvest a tree that has grown for years, only to have it produce inferior lumber.

What a waste of time and resources. How tragic it is when we see a life wasted. Precious time is wasted pursuing treasures that have no eternal value. Selfishness keeps us from sharing and giving compassion to those who are in need. Bitterness is fed daily until it sours everything we touch. These are branches that divert our energy away from our main purpose, to live the life that God has blessed us with and to glorify Him. We need to rid our lives of these branches. Stop feeding them. Begin to grow good useable wood over the scars. Drop them to the forest floor where they can rot away and feed the local termites. But how do we do this?

BIBLES, BEAVERS, AND BIG TIMBER

The industrious timber manager will often resort to pruning. The goal here is to physically remove the lower branches, usually on the first eighteen feet of the tree trunk, in order to begin the process of growing clear wood over the knots. This is best, if done by others, and even better if it is free. Often a local forestry school will have a group of students eager to work in the great outdoors. Many an accountant has been born after a good day with a limb saw.

When I was in college, I was required to spend an afternoon doing just that—providing free labor in the name of education. It involved using the above-mentioned limb saw, and applying it to those branches that had refused to fall off on their own within a stand of red pine trees. While pruning is drastic, it is effective.

In Matthew 5, Jesus tells of the need to prune our lives. He states that if our eyes are causing us to sin, get rid of them before they drag us to hell. Likewise with our hands, he said it was better to go through life with one hand than go to hell with two. Now Christ was not advocating that we literally poke out our eyes, but what he was saying is that we need to be willing to apply some serious pruning.

To prune our lives means we have to rid ourselves of the branches that cause knots. Sometimes it means making a committed effort to change a habit, to adjust a portion of our life that is not pleasing to God. It might call for more drastic action. If making a commitment to do the right thing doesn't seem to work, take drastic measures. Having trouble with watching the wrong TV programs? Maybe you need to get rid of the TV. Having trouble watching raunchy movies? Get rid of the DVD. Wasting time with the video games? Toss them. Playing sports keeps you from ministering to someone in need? Drop out of the league. Harboring a grudge? Try going to the person and asking for forgiveness. Don't hang on to those branches. The end result is not worth it. What a tragedy to live a life, only to find out at the end of it, those branches have made you virtually worthless, or worse yet, that those branches will keep you from entering heaven.

Just as branches can help to define a tree, to give it an identifying characteristic, the things we do give us an identity and character. But be careful. The branches supporting a tree are predominately in the upper portion of the tree, gathering in the sunlight, producing necessary elements for survival. Test your branches. Are they in the "Sonlight?" Is Jesus, God's only begotten Son, pleased with them? Are they providing the critical elements in your life? If not, drop those branches, or pick up the pruning saw. It truly is a matter of life and death, and a matter of eternal life.

Colossians 3 is perhaps the "knot" chapter of the Bible. Here the Apostle Paul gives a pretty good listing of the good and bad branches. In talking to Christians (verse 1), he gives a list of what to get rid of and what to keep. Branches that cause knots and need to be pruned are found in verses 5 through 9a:

"Therefore put to death your members which are on the earth: fornication, uncleanness, passion, evil desire, and covetousness, which is idolatry. Because of these things the wrath of God is coming upon the sons of disobedience, in which you yourselves once walked when you lived in them. But now you yourselves are to put off all these: anger, wrath, malice, blasphemy, filthy language out of your mouth. Do not lie to one another, ..."

Branches to keep are found in verses 10 through 17. They include showing: *mercy, humbleness, forgiveness, and love.* The Christian, whether man, woman, boy, or girl who has asked Jesus into their heart, knows what is expected of them. They can test each branch against this portion of scripture. But the unsaved, the person who has yet to seek God's free gift of salvation, they stand with all of their branches. They have held on to each one. They continue to grow in an awkward and unnatural way, with branches dominating the bottom of their trunk. They have produced no fruit, nothing of value. They have refused to shed the branch of self and surrender their life to Jesus. In a parable Jesus said such a tree would be cut down and used for firewood (Luke 3:9). That puts it rather bluntly don't you think.

BIBLES, BEAVERS, AND BIG TIMBER

Noah was called to build a boat out of wood. The purpose was to save all who would heed God's call. The boat was perfect, and knot-free. What a tragedy that only eight people heeded the call and the rest perished. God is still looking for some knot-free wood today. There are boats to be built, people to be rescued. Are you ready to shed some branches, and surrender to the Master Carpenter?

Identity Theft

You are probably wondering how the topic of identity theft fits into the whole forestry setting. I suppose we could talk about the forester who loses his wallet in the woods; someone else picks it up, and then they go on a buying spree. Actually, I believe I have seen that very thing, minus the forestry setting, on a few commercials lately. The idea of someone assuming the identity of another is not new. As long as there has been a theater, folks have been donning the mask and traits of others to tell a story, or to convince the audience they are in fact someone else.

The forester must battle this idea of identity theft every day they are in the woods. Here's how it works. When looking at a stand of timber, the forester does several things, all to one common end, answering the question of, "What is the timber worth?" To accomplish this mission, he takes measurements of the tree diameters at a specific point above the ground, and the height of the trees in question. He also must judge the amount of a given product that can be taken from the trees. He can do all of these things to the tree because he can see and touch it. He can apply measuring tapes and use various optical devices that allow him to calculate important numbers used in determining how much the timber is worth.

Here is where the identity issue comes into play. The forester—unless he is from Smallville and goes by the name Clark Kent—cannot see "into" the tree. The portion of the tree that resides behind the bark is what he is really after, but he cannot see it. To try to overcome this obstacle, the forester may employ several methods of semi-divination. He may, if he has wrists of iron, seek to bore the tree. (I sometimes believe the best way to do this is to tell stories of my childhood.) It certainly is better than using what is called an increment borer. The increment borer is a long, hollow, drill bit that the forester must drill into the tree by hand. By doing this he is able to remove a core sample from the tree; whereby he can judge the age of the tree, the density of the growth rings, and if fortunate, he can ascertain the presence of rot. Finding a tree's age and density can be of great benefit in determining the value of the trees in question. The older and denser the wood, the more it has value. But knowing the true identity of the timber is about knowing whether it has the dreaded rot within it. That is the key. Nothing is more tragic than to assume you have purchased a beautiful stand of oak, only to find the logs coming to the deck are hollow and full of rot. Pass the crying towel, because these trees are not even worth half of what you paid.

Besides rot, the forester is wondering about worms, insects, and the presence of wind shake. Any of these things can cause a serious degradation to the value of the timber. You see, trees do not always show these signs outwardly. They appear to be sound, in good shape, but when the pressure of the saw mill comes against them, or when the ax is laid to the trunk, all is revealed.

In II Corinthians 5, the Apostle Paul is writing to Christians, to those who have asked Jesus to save them. He writes in verse 10:

For we must all appear before the judgment seat of Christ, that each one may receive the things done in the body, according to what he has done, whether good or bad.

This is pretty important if you claim to be a Christian. It means that there is coming a time when what's behind the bark will be made known. Were you sold out for Jesus, or did you simply sell out? Were you sincere in your efforts to share the Love of Christ with others, or did you deem others unworthy of your time? Did you have the time and desire to help those less fortunate? Were you Jesus to someone else?

Just as those trees can hide a potential problem, there will come a time when the truth is known—the buzz of the chainsaw, the pop of the ax, or maybe it will be the piercing bit of the increment borer. But in the end, the true value of the tree will be determined, and a suitable use for it will be found. How much sound wood will be found in your life? Will you be in the kitchen as a fine cabinet, meeting the needs of people with the gifts that God has given you; or maybe a piano in the parlor, refreshing the souls of the weary with songs of praise, or will you be in a little vase, just a collection of toothpicks?

Standing

He stood guard, a watchman on the wall, surveying the land.

The wind was really blowing. It was going to be a black night in the swamp, yet again. He had seen many such nights in his 250 years. Often they had raged throughout the swamp, storms with names, and many more without. Even now, just the thought of some of those storms would cause him to again get the "shakes." They would come from all directions, during all seasons. Pushing, pulling. The autumn storms, such as this, were the worst. Having survived the long hot summer, he was too heavy to withstand the strain. He needed to shed some weight before winter, but he preferred to do it on his own; and there was time yet to prepare for winter. While tonight the winds moaned, he knew that in the morning things would be better. He had weathered them all before, but not by anything he had done. It was the ground that his Creator had prepared for him; firm, deep rich soil, just right for putting down roots. And the Creator had done it all for him, prepared this beautiful little spot for him well in advance of his arrival.

In the darkness he reflected on "That Storm," and shuddered. What a storm it had been, and so long ago. The wind was fierce then too, and the rain was coming in sheets. Trees crashed in the dark all around him, branches shattering and screaming in the wind. He had held on as tight to his mother as he could, but he could feel with each gust a weakening of the tie that bound them together.

Her words still echoed in his mind and heart, "Don't be afraid, the Creator has prepared something special for you, now you be special for him. Grow where you are planted. Reach for the sky; lift up your branches to the Creator. Don't get sidetracked and grow branches that do not reach upward. They will fail you in the day of trial, and pull you down. Strive to always grow, for when you stop, you will begin to decay, first within, then without."

BIBLES, BEAVERS, AND BIG TIMBER

No sooner had she spoken those words to him, than a violent gust tore him from her. Downward he plunged, towards the ground he had always strived to stay above. He had always imagined it to be firm and strong, but not on this night. The water was tearing under the tree, the current rushing off into the night with a purpose only it could understand. With a flash of lightning, another tree in the forest erupted into a shower of sparks, and in that brief moment of light, he saw the last of the tree that had been his home, his shelter for his entire existence. And with a rush of water and gravity, his adventure began. Bobbing and careening through the darkness, bouncing from unseen objects, absorbing blows that he never saw coming. They seemed to tear at his very being, as if the terror of this night would separate him from his very life. Would that be the purpose the Creator had planned for him?

Where am I headed? Why am I in this storm? The questions raced through his mind even as he rushed onward amidst the raging current. Soon he stopped bouncing off of tree trunks and realized he must be out in the river. He had watched that river from his perch on the hill all summer, lazily flowing towards the sunrise. On it he had seen the birds float and the fish splash. Now it was his turn. He began to ponder his predicament. He was after all a white oak, even though still in acorn form. He was suited for dry ground, high ground; ground without water. Yet how could his Creator have a plan for him? Surely he must have made a mistake. Maybe the storm caught him by surprise. He began to panic. His life was over. A passing duck would scoop him up, and that would be it—some life, some purpose.

The dawn finally broke. The peaceful river was a boiling cauldron with red dirt and debris: trees, logs, branches. He wasn't the only one who had had a bad night. However, the company didn't make him feel any better. As he floated he watched the changing landscape. The hills were disappearing. In their place were towering palisades, growing in the water. He had never seen such a thing. But he had heard the tales. Trees that kept their leaves year round and never touched dry ground. What could be happening to him? The Creator had let him slip through his fingers after all. He wasn't meant to have landed in the water, and certainly not to drift into this groundless, waterlogged terrain. With a downcast spirit he floated on. Despair pulled at him. His world was crashing down around him. Had the Creator failed him, or had it all been just a tale?

Night came and went. The river was so much wider, and was noticeably slower. But still no hills were in sight. The current began to push him slowly towards the sunset side of the river. The palisades were menacing. He drifted from the sunlight of the river into the shadow of the timber and soon the darkness of the deep woods. But not like the woods he knew. Here instead of ground was water and current, yet everywhere there were trees.

This must be the swamp he thought—the world of cypress and tupelo. He had heard of it; been warned of it. There were dangers here—shallow dirt, flooding, and dare he think it...beavers! In his weariness he drifted into sleep. "Trust the Creator," he mumbled to himself.

When he awoke, he was surprised to find that he was no longer floating on the current of the flood. He had been deposited on what looked like a small bump. A little plot of ground, still wet from the receding flood, but a bump none-the-less. Tentatively he stuck out a foot, expecting to feel mud, but instead felt sand. How could it be? How could the soil here, in this swamp, be anything but mud?

His mother's word returned, "Grow where the Creator places you." It didn't make sense to him, but what choice did he have? At least he was out of the water. And so the process had begun. Year upon year, he dug his roots deeper and deeper into the moist soil. His bump was barely wider than his branches. The deep water of the swamp started just past his drip line. He began to flourish, year after year. Remembering his mother's words, he kept his branches pushing upward. Soon he was producing fruit, little acorns of his own. He began to look forward to those autumn days each year, when the deer and turkey would come from beyond, anxious for his treats. And over the years he had watched the hunters come for those deer and turkey. First they were clad in loincloths, and then buckskin, and recently in cloth that would often remind him of old friends. They would all gather on his bump. And he in turn, thankful for the company, would provide needed shade. Here on the little hill, he was a refuge for the passer-by, a chance for them to get out of the swamp.

With a start he came back to the present. The howling of the storm was getting louder. He heard groans coming from the forest around him, and watched as branches and leaves were ripped from him. He sensed that perhaps this time it was different. He felt a longing to rest. The storms didn't scare him as much as they used to. He had learned to trust the Creator. After all, He had created this little hill. The Creator had to have been preparing it for years, before he was even swinging on a branch. How many storms had it taken to build it, to wash the sand and clay from his homeland to this spot, in the middle of a swamp? And yet He had. And He had brought the storm that night as well, a storm that seemed to tear at his very faith. And just when he had given up, he was here. And he had flourished, and prospered at the task given to him by the Creator.

All things must come to an end he thought. He could feel it now. The roots were giving way. Slowly but surely, with every sway, he could feel them pulling lose from the soil they had held for so long. The Creator doesn't make mistakes he thought. He has proven Himself to me all these years.

The wind was screaming, it was unlike any that he had heard before. His own acorns were being dragged from his branches. He shouted out words of encouragement, words that he himself had been told—words that time and trials had proven to be true. The pressure now was immense. He fought against it as it pushed him, dragging him towards the ground. One more gust, a gust as hard as any he had endured for the past two and a half centuries, and he surrendered. The branches he had so carefully managed throughout the years softened his fall, but fall he did. It was over. A once great giant, towering into the sky, now lay prone. The wind still ravaged the woods, seeking new victims. But it was over for him. The wind could not harm him now.

He knew the Creator was still in control, and besides, there was going to be a vacancy on the little hill, and who knew what might come floating in with the morning sunrise.

Psalms 1:3 *He shall be like a tree planted by the rivers of water, that brings forth its fruit in its season, whose leaf also shall not wither; and whatever he does shall prosper.*

Isaiah 61:3b *"...that they may be called trees of righteousness, the planting of the Lord, that He may be glorified."*

*** In memory of a 250-year old white oak, found growing on a little bump in the middle of a tupelo swamp along the Roanoke River. It was all alone on its hill. It had twenty feet of perfect log before the first branch. No rot of any kind. It was blown over by Hurricane Isabel, September 2003. The root ball was thirty feet wide. An attempt was made to salvage it by helicopter, but even the smallest useable log was too heavy for the helicopter to lift. I look forward to visiting the hill again to look for sprouts in the future.

Salvage

Hear the word *mayhem* and certain memories may come to mind—the time you had twelve five-year olds in the church nursery, maybe a birthday party at Chucky Cheese, or perhaps the time you accidentally hit the motorcycles parked at the bar next to the laundry mat. Regardless of what the picture is, you recognize mayhem when you see it. I have been walking in mayhem lately. As is the case in the Southeast Coastal Plain of these United States, every fall we have one of those "weather events." Now I used to think that the Weather Channel created all of this stuff just to keep people glued to the TV, but after going through several hurricanes, I too dial in when something with a name is lurking off of the East Coast. Hurricanes are wrecking machines. First it is the bands of rain. We are talking about water falling. It usually starts a day or two prior to the actual arrival of the storm. The rain has the effect of soaking the ground; which if you are in the tree harvesting or growing business, is not always a good thing. As the ground becomes saturated, the roots of the trees lose their ability to cling to the soil, and then you have a situation. This situation is worsened by the arrival of the next element of the storm, the wind. Quietly humming along at 35 mph, it lulls you into thinking that the storm is just so much hub-bub. You check the Weather Channel to find out the storm is still four hours away. Oh...

When the winds hit, the trees begin to do calisthenics, leaning to the left, back to the right, and down, then up. What a work out. Staring out from the window, you can quickly become mesmerized by the howling and swaying trees, as well a pine cones flying; also branches slamming into the house, and squirrels hanging on by their toenails. What a sight! In the woods, it is even worse—swaying trees slamming into other trees, breaking branches, and knocking off bark. Leaves are also falling like all the autumn days rolled into one. And just when it looks like the storm will pass and the forest will survive, it happens—mayhem. The first soldier falls. One of the grand old trees on the edge, one that has been taking the brunt of the storm and defending the stand against the full assault force of the storm, has surrendered. Seemingly in slow motion, its roots having lost their ability to hold the saturated soil any longer, the tree crashes. As it goes, the smaller trees under its canopy have no chance. They are crushed. Roots are blown out of the ground, stems shattered. Then the mayhem begins. Unabated into the stand, the wind and the saturated soil become a gruesome twosome, and the trees begin to topple—falling, splintering, tops exploding, roots throwing mud into the air. The sound, if it could be heard above the roar of the wind, would be frightening. Amidst the moaning of the wind can also be heard the gunshot sound of snapping stems and busting branches.

After the storm, the scene is not pretty. Trees lie in twisted clumps with their roots raised to the sky in surrender, surrendering to the forces that conspired to cause their destruction. Everywhere trees lay in piles of mud, water, limbs; in short, mayhem.

At this point, the forester is faced with a monster of a task—salvage. He must find someone to enter the tract, and log the timber that is lying in twisted and mangled fashion on the ground, or partially on the ground, or at a severe lean. It is dangerous work. Trees under tension can snap in a variety of directions. Saws bind, equipment sinks, and all-the-while the clock is running, the clock of time. You see with their roots exposed and their branches on the ground, these trees are facing death. Their lifeline has been mortally crushed. As such, the inevitable process of decay will soon begin. Failure to harvest the timber quickly will result in its loss of value, and very soon it will have grown all those years for nothing. It will soon become worthless debris.

Mark chapter 5, is a story of mayhem. If you could describe the life of a person in terms of a stand of trees, and then throw in a category four hurricane, you would have the man whom Jesus encountered in a countryside known as Gadarenes. Here He met a man with an unclean spirit, according to verse 2. Let's read the particulars:

Home was the local graveyard...

He could not be bound...

He had broken out of fetters and chains...

He had no peace...

He would scream throughout the night, and the day...

He would cut himself, abusing his body...

This man was living, walking, mayhem. And he was dying. Sin was in control of his life. James 1:15 tells us that sin brings death. And yet into this scene of mayhem, comes a salvage logger. Someone who is willing to enter into the mayhem, and seek to salvage what still has value. This man in the Gadara had value. No one else thought so, but Jesus did. Others ran from this man, others tried to bind him, but Jesus came to him. He salvaged him. He harvested him before death and sin could. Before the decay of sin could completely destroy him, Jesus brought life. This man's mayhem turned into peace. Verse 15 states that after his meeting with Jesus, he was changed, changed so much that he actually becomes a missionary.

Jesus tells him in verse 19, "Go home to your friends, and tell them what great things the Lord hath done for you, and how He has had compassion on you." Salvage work begins with compassion. In seeing value even when mayhem is in control. Compassion doesn't like to lose, it is always moving forward, seeking, finding a way to reach out.

Is your life in mayhem, sin controlled and decaying? There is one who seeks, one who believes you have value, one who can salvage you. The best thing the wild man did is found at the beginning of the story; he came running to Jesus. In which direction are you headed?

Games

When you think of games and forests, what comes to mind? If you are an avid watcher of ESPN you might think of the various logging games they show where folks chop and saw and climb various tree parts for cash prizes and bragging rights. There are chain saws that have been mated with motorcycle engines, huge double bit axes that you could shave with, and lots and lots of sawdust. Others might think of games that come from the wood produced by the forest. Baseball bats and basketball floors would qualify as wood products. And how about that wooden pegboard they used to have at the school gym, the ones that you always wanted to climb, but not when anyone was around?!

At a smaller level, there are the wooden games you might have in your house. We have a checkerboard, a chess set, a cribbage board, and bead game from Africa. Each of these games has a wooden board upon which some game of skill is to be played. Let's look at these a little closer. The checkerboard, is a flat board with painted or stained crosshatches. Upon this board one can play checkers—the game of children, grandparents, hungry customers waiting for their tables to be ready, and of course Barney and Andy at the courthouse. Checkers at its base level is a game of strategy where one player strives to defeat another.

Chess is basically checkers with a college degree. Cribbage is a card game, heavy on the math. The wooden board here is elongated, with numerous holes drilled in it—sort of like the school pegboard. These holes are for counting points, creating a racetrack effect on the board, with the winner finishing first. The bead game, Mancala, is also an elongated board, with little depressions, each large enough to hold several beads. It also serves as a racetrack.

Games, we are compelled to play games! We like to compete, to win. The essence of the game is to win. In order to win we must commit ourselves to some strategy, or we leave it up to chance. Certainly, many a savings account has been left to chance on the gaming tables of Las Vegas.

In order to win, we often must become focused on the goal. We have to ignore the distractions. My youngest son found out very quickly that if he can talk me into chess or checkers while I am watching a basketball game, then his chances of winning increase drastically. We take our games very seriously. Ask the college football coach who wins eight out of ten, yet finds himself on the unemployment line.

Perhaps playing games and the forest have more in common than we might at first think. Games are played in the forest, and the products from the forest are used to create games. It would seem the two have always been together.

One day a game was played at the foot of a "tree":

John 19:23,24 Then the soldiers, when they had crucified Jesus, took His garments and made four parts, to each soldier a part, and also the tunic. Now the tunic was without seam, woven from the top in one piece. They said therefore among themselves, "Let us not tear it, but cast lots for it..."

Can you picture this scene? Jesus Christ, the Son of God, has been nailed to a cross. He hangs above you, bleeding, and you decide it's time for a game, and out comes the dice. Someone is going to win a new robe. What a tragic comment on these men. To play a game at the foot of the cross, while above you the owner of the prize, the one who only recently wore the robe, and he is dying. He is in fact dying an excruciating death. The noise, the crowd, the smell—none of this matters; there is a prize to be won, a game to be played.

Tragically, the game is still being played. The dice are still being rolled. The chances are still being taken. Let's ignore Jesus. Let's shut him out. Let's play a game, and all the while, Jesus died for you. There are two types of games being played at the foot of that cross, even today. One is a game of strategy. One where we are willing to acknowledge God, even to call upon Him for salvation, but we aren't willing to give Him Lordship of our life. We run around the board shouting, "King Me!" wanting to be the winner, wanting all the credit. The other game is one of chance. That somehow we can win our way into heaven, without accepting the sacrifice of Christ, without surrendering our souls and our lives to Him. We look up at the cross; we see the robe; and we roll the dice. Maybe we can win the robe, and look like Jesus, and that will be enough.

Titus 3:5 *...not by works of righteousness which we have done, but according to His mercy He saved us...*

Ephesians 2:8,9 *For by grace you have been saved through faith; and that not of yourselves; it is the gift of God, not of works, lest anyone should boast.*

We cannot possibly find salvation in our own merit, by our own strategy, or by chance. Neither can we claim Jesus to be our savior if He is not also our LORD. It is right there in front of us. It's made of wooden boards, but it isn't a game; it's a cross. It's all about life. A life that is full and victorious, and surrendered to Jesus. Crown Him today.

Let's Take a Cruise

Many of you have just raced into your memory vault. Julie and Gopher are showing you to your cabin; the band is playing a Jamaican beach song; the waves are gently slapping the ship; the breeze is soft and you are in love.

Or maybe the flash back is to a particular car, a real cherry. One that on Saturday nights you could be found in, driving through the local neighborhood. In the little southern town my mother grew up in, such a ritual existed. Local teens would drive the mile and a half distance from one end of town to the other. At one end was the school parking lot, and at the other was a carwash. Beyond the city limits was 30 miles of rice and cotton fields, and not much else. So the cruisers drive back and forth, back and forth. To this day you can still drive the strip, just get in line.

But the cruise I want to take you on today is one I have alluded to before, a timber cruise. It will involve quite a bit of effort, walking for the most part. Running is involved if we find ground bees, snakes, hornet nests; or we decide to eat any meal from cans purchased at a local gas station. The cruise is essentially a means used to evaluate a particular piece of forested property. An examination, if you will, of the trees and land. Why are we doing it? What value does the property have? Where are the problems? What could be done to make it more valuable? These are the questions to be solved by our cruise.

First the "why?" Why would we want to leave a perfectly comfortable truck, with working air conditioning, to go walking in the woods? There are mosquitoes out there, and yellow flies are lining up outside the window, anxiously awaiting the opening of the door. The heat will increase ten extra degrees as soon as you step into the forest, and that gentle breeze that was blowing this morning at the office, is ready to quit as soon as you begin.

BIBLES, BEAVERS, AND BIG TIMBER

It is against this background that we must determine how bad do we want to answer the question "why?" You see, we determine to cruise a tract because we want to know what it is worth; and if it is land, we manage, then what can be done to make it more valuable. If we have an investment to protect or to draw a return from, then it will help us make the right decisions if we know all we can about it.

Thus we need to take a cruise. While on this cruise, we will look at the timber. Now trees have several attributes that we will need to be aware of. The first and perhaps most important is the species. (What kind of tree it is.) In one of my college classes, we once took a hike to identify trees by flashlight. It was important for us, as foresters, to be able to identify trees species simply by the distinct bark patterns they have. Forget the leaves on the trees, or on the ground, because in the woods such things will often be useless. Leaves are so high up they are too small to see, and the branches all mix together from neighboring trees. It is important to know if a tree is an ash or a sweet gum.

Recently, I had a group of lumberjacks from the Western states cutting for me, and they were not familiar with the two aforementioned species. Now the price for ash lumber is very high, while sweet gum is sold as very low-grade lumber, and sells for very little. In the woods, to an untrained eye, it is very easy to mix the two up at times. These lumberjacks could not distinguish the ash from the sweet gum, and were constantly cutting the wrong trees. Needless to say, when we started getting useless logs delivered to the landing, we had to hold a quick "tree identity" session. From then on, trees cut down that turned out to be the wrong species, received a large wedge cut in the middle of the log, a sign to the skidding crew to leave the tree in the woods. It was a sign of value.

Variations can also occur within a species, such as with oaks. There are over fifteen different varieties of red oak, and they are important ones. Cherry bark red oak or northern red is much more valuable than water oak or scarlet oak. It will behoove us then to look honestly at the trees. Call a gum a gum, and an ash an ash. Mixing them up will cause a drastic consequence when the value of the tract becomes known.

Since we have determined the tree species present, we then must look closer at these trees and determine if they are indeed the real things. The outside of the tree only tells part of the story. What the lumberman is after is not the bark, but the wood underneath it; and it must have enough quality to allow its value to be fully realized. Yet there are few guarantees to this!

Inside the tree may be worms, gnawing little tunnels through the wood. Or perhaps rot and decay have crept in. The tree looks solid, looks healthy, but when the sawmill splits it open or the logger cuts it from the stump, the awful truth leaps out—hollow.

While there are a few tricks to finding some of these before purchasing the trees, there is no fool-proof method. The strong-armed forester can attempt to drill some of the trees, but he can only do this to a few of the trees. Some folks carry a hammer and strike the trees, attempting to hear a hollow ring. Perhaps an area has a history, and some caution as to history repeating itself can be employed.

Buyers of cypress are often ecstatic to find stands of the valuable yet scarce trees, only to be disappointed when they arrive at the mill to find the presence of wind shake—a malady that cannot be detected sometimes until the boards themselves are being sawn. Thus in reality, the truth is known only after the tree is cut. Is it real and genuine, or a pretender?

Another goal of the cruise is in finding potential problems within the stand. Beetles and moths top the list of insect pests that can quickly devastate a stand of timber. Trees under stress are greatly susceptible to pests that can kill. Exotic plants and fungus, transported by vectors such as wind or animals, can destroy hundreds of acres of timber.

And of course, the ever-popular beaver adds to the list of potential problems that can destroy standing

BIBLES, BEAVERS, AND BIG TIMBER

timber. Finding such timber predators requires a response. Identifying the invaders, but taking no action, will likely result in no timber. But often such ventures are costly. They involve sacrifice and expense. Some may choose to keep the invaders, and hope for the best; but in the long run they lose more than they save.

Finally, the true value of the timber is set by what it will produce. What products will be made from the wood? Compare the cost of a roll of toilet paper to the cost of a sixteen-foot two by ten, and you can see what I mean. Some trees can produce the wood to make valuable products such as high quality lumber, but how many of those trees are present?

Psalm 26 records a cruise performed by David. One where he decides to examine where he is and what value he might have. In verse 1 he asks to be judged (vindicated), and in verse 2, he implores of the Lord to examine his life, to test him and determine his value.

Vindicate me, O Lord, for I have walked in mine integrity. I have also trusted in the Lord; I shall not slip. Examine me, O Lord, and prove me; try my mind and my heart.

What a thought. David wanted to know how he stood before God. What was in his life that was good and valuable, and what was in his life that needed to be fixed. He calls for a cruise, an evaluation, an examination.

In verses 3-5, David explores the question of truth in his life. Can it be seen and identified?

For Your loving kindness is before my eyes, and I have walked in Your truth. I have not sat with idolatrous mortals, nor will I go in with hypocrites. I have hated the assembly of evildoers, and will not sit with the wicked.

It would seem to me that David is looking to stay with the right company. He is examining his surroundings, who he is with, and who he might be looking like. Experience tells us that we take on the characteristics of those around us. Truth has an appearance of its own, it needs to be distinct; it must be distinct, otherwise truth will be confused and covered.

Verses 6-8 speak of purity, of being sound and sincere, not false, not full of rot.

I will wash my hands in innocence; so I will go about Your altar, O Lord, that I may proclaim with the voice of thanksgiving, and tell of all Your wondrous works. Lord, I have loved the habitation of Your house, and the place where Your glory dwells.

The Lord wants his followers to have hands of innocence, to have a voice that speaks with thanksgiving and praise, not a voice of hypocrisy and deceit. The outside package is ultimately graded by what it produces from the inside.

In the closing verses of this Psalm, David writes of being used. He desires to be a man of integrity, a man redeemed, and a recipient of God's mercy. He wanted to stand on even footing before his fellow man and bless the Lord. He wanted to be a man that could make a difference.

The purpose of the cruise is to examine, to find the value, and to identify the problems. It is not an easy request. Satan would prefer we not get out of the truck. It might get too hot, too uncomfortable. If you ask the Lord to look you over, you had best be ready for the reply. The Lord is looking for men, women, boys, and girls who are genuine, who are not afraid to look like Christians on the outside, and who are pure Christians on the inside, with no rot, no decay. They cannot be pretenders, nor have wedges cut to show them as being unusable.

Are we willing to clear our lives of the pests and predators that seek to destroy us?

Are we willing to remove the filth of the world and its indifference to truth?

Will we toss out the deceit and selfishness? They line up at the door, waiting to enter our lives, to find some means of entrance to slip in and destroy our usefulness.

The Lord will show those areas to us. The question is, will we clear them out? Will we accept the cost and inconvenience?

Why? That we might have a purpose, that we might have value in the eyes of the One who loves us, who sent

BIBLES, BEAVERS, AND BIG TIMBER

His Son to die for us. There is a reason for it all. It is to be used by the Owner of the forest, to produce that which He desires, for His good pleasure.

II Peter 3:14 *Therefore, beloved, looking forward to these things, be diligent to be found by Him in peace, without spot and blameless...*

Cypress Ponds

While hacking my way through a dense jungle of brush and blown-over trees, I came upon a "beaver kill." Such a sight tends to be a bit depressing. Common to most "beaver kills" are the hollow remains of once stately trees: trees that had grown for over half a century, trees just reaching their prime. Now they stood as shadows of their former selves. Limbs had fallen off. Bark was loose and hanging. Birds and insects had been meeting for lunch all along the trunk, leaving large gaping holes staring vacantly across the desolate landscape. They were not made for this.

They were once growing happily, pushing towards the sky. At night they dreamed about fine furniture and pianos. Then the intruders came. Intruders who were not happy with the way the forest looked. Intruders who sought to change the scene to their own advantage. And they did. Little by little the water table beneath the tree roots began to rise. The rain that fell did not leave the area, or soak into the ground like it once did. At first the trees shook it off. Sometimes there was just too much water, just like sometimes there was too little water. But it had become routine now. The smallest amount of rain caused the water to increase around their roots. Soon it never left, and just continued a slow progression up the trunk. The trees tried desperately to soak up the water into their roots, but it was too much. The water was choking off the oxygen supply. The tall trees, towering into the air, were suffocating. Leaves began to fall off, yet autumn was months away. Without the leaves, the trees began to starve. In their weakened state, insects showed up, hungrily devouring the cellulose fibers. Then they were dead. No fine furniture. No piano.

Beaver kills have always made me sad. Nature has a way of being rather blunt and brutal. I continued with my journey, sloshing through the stagnant water, until suddenly I was confronted with trees again, large trees and they were alive. They were also standing deep in the water. Why were these trees able to survive the water, while their brethren across the pond could not?

The answer can be summed up as follows: they used their "knees." Yes, these trees were cypress trees. Cypress trees, while very capable of growing on ground not covered with water, also do very well when the water gets deep. They can actually flourish. How do they do it? This question has nagged at foresters for years, but it all seems to point to the knees. These knees appear to be some sort of root, sprouting upward, often sticking up several feet from the forest floor, sticking above the water. Scientists believe that these roots perform some sort of air exchange, allowing the tree to breath.

We can find a cypress tree in Psalm 61. In it the psalmist is in dire straits. Read verse 2:

From the end of the earth I will cry to You, when my heart is overwhelmed; lead me to the rock that is higher than I.

Troubles, like beavers, can swim into our lives. At first, it would appear that we can survive, but slowly the troubles begin to multiply. The sickness lingers longer than expected. Complications arise. Perhaps a job is lost, a spouse wanders, a child rebels. Troubles come.

If you have spent any time in Sunday school, you will know that whatever questions the teacher may ask, if you answer with either "Jesus, prayer, or faith," you will have a good chance of being right. Sometimes we have trouble fitting these simple answers into the questions of life. I think the psalmist would agree. Look at Psalm 61 again.

Verse 1: *Hear my cry, O God; attend to my prayer.*

Verse 2: *...I will cry to You...*

The problem with Sunday school answers is that we often do not actually expect them to work. They are just answers. When we are no longer coloring the Apostle Peter in a fishing boat, we tend to discount what we learned in Sunday school. How tragic!

The scene shows the psalmist overwhelmed with troubles. That is real, and not make-believe. Troubles will come upon us, and usually to such an extent that we will be in danger of being overwhelmed. To be overwhelmed means to have it over your head, to have more than you can handle. Like the trees with the water over their roots, when we are overwhelmed, we face a grave danger—one of suffocating. We lose the very essence of life, and slowly die, losing the value that we have worked for and accumulated over the years.

Like the cypress, we need to learn how to survive when the troubles of life seem to overwhelm us; we need to get above our troubles. Continuing in Psalm 61:

Verse 2: *...lead me to the rock that is higher than I.*

Verse 3: *For You have been a shelter for me, a strong tower from the enemy.*

David knows that prayer gives him a chance to look above his troubles, to focus on God instead of on his problems. He learns from his prayers that God is aware of his situation, and that while God may not be ready to deliver him out of his situation, He can make it bearable. Here is how:

Verse 4a: *I will abide in Your tabernacle...*

David must stay near to God. We do that when we are on our knees.

Verse 4b: *...I will trust in the shelter of Your wings.*

David must submit to God. You cannot stay under God's wing if you have plans to go a different direction.

Cypress trees can grow where other trees cannot because God gave them the means and ability to survive, to even flourish. He gave them knees. He has done no less for us. We too have been given the tools to survive the difficulties of life. We have been given prayer. Draw close to God, submit to His wing, and accept His direction. And not only can we survive—but we can grow and flourish, and provide God with a valuable servant.

Food Piles

Have you ever heard the old saying, "Water, water, everywhere, and not a drop to drink?" I do not like water in my woods. That is water, where water is not supposed to be. I was doing a routine check on a stand of timber that bordered a notorious beaver stream one day. Beavers had seemed to materialize from out of nowhere, and dammed the stream. Now it had been a few months since I had been in to check this area, thus finding an active dam was not a surprise. Finding a fresh food pile next to the lodge was a bit of a disappointment, however.

Food piles are what beavers create when they are getting ready for the winter. It wasn't that the beavers were active that caused me to frown, but rather that winter was approaching. When winter approaches, even in the South, along with it comes ice. I don't much care for ice, especially since it has to get cold to make it. Too much time has passed since the days of my childhood, and I have lost my enthusiasm for cold weather.

The beaver sets about building a food pile next to his lodge just in case the ice gets thick, and just in case it lasts a while. You see, a food pile is a collection of sticks and small trees that a beaver will cut off and float to his lodge. Once there he makes a floating pile or mat. These sticks will be accessible from under the water, under the ice, allowing the beaver to have a meal when the pond or swamp is frozen over, and he cannot find a hole to climb out of. Since he keeps all of his lodge entrances under water, a frozen pond means he is trapped at home or at least under the water surrounding his home—thus the food pile.

Now consider for a moment a delinquent beaver. He is distracted. He knows winter is coming, and there is a need to gather supplies. Failure to prepare could be a capital offense, causing the death of himself or his family. He decides to get busy with the food pile.

At first all goes well. He has found several juicy cottonwood saplings, and some willow was growing just upstream. But then he saw something else. It was magnificent and awesome. He had to have it on his food pile. He would be the envy of all. He began to gnaw and chew. It was tough all right, but what a beauty. Finally he had it on his pile. Yes, it was tall and slender, and had a single bright, green "leaf" on the top, with the word "Johnson Road" on it. It did look good on his food pile.

Eager to add to the diversity of his pile, he began to look further and further from the lodge. He returned late one evening with a tall, spindly looking pole, it did not have any leaves, but it was shiny. He wondered what the man meant when he heard him screaming across the yard about a TV antenna?

Yes, he soon had a mighty fine food pile, only there wasn't much food on it. He did have several street signs, the TV antenna, a mailbox and post, and two orange traffic cones. The beaver had become distracted. He had spent his time pursuing items that would not help him when the cold days of winter came. When the swamp would freeze over and he was trapped under the ice, he could swim around and look at the bright green leaf declaring, "Johnson Road," but it made for tough eating.

What a silly beaver we would say. He knew winter was coming. He was busy. But why didn't he prepare?

Winter comes to us all. Life begins to slow down and takes on a bit of a chill. The joints don't move like they used to. The hair, if it stays, changes to a gray color. Yes winter is always at the end of autumn, after the summer days are just a memory. Winter reminds us that we are mortal. Life as we know it is just the beginning of an eternal journey, and the "death of winter" is the stepping from this life on earth to life in eternity. Life doesn't end it just changes requirements.

Food piles are where we lay up supplies for the coming winter. Jesus said it like this in Matthew 6:19-21

"Do not lay up for yourselves treasures on earth, where moth and rust destroy and where thieves break in and steal; but lay up for yourselves treasures in heaven, where neither moth nor rust destroys and where thieves do

not break in and steal. For where your treasure is, there your heart will be also."

Are we building our "food piles," the supplies to see us through the upcoming winter, with items of junk? Perhaps we are collecting things that may look pretty, that may take great time and energy to acquire? But at the end, when that icy hand of death takes hold of us, what will we have? Just as a solid food pile will allow a beaver to survive the winter, laying up treasure in heaven will allow us to survive the winter, and allow us to live in heaven.

Looking for something good to place on the pile, some choice cottonwood perhaps? Try some of Colossians 3:12-17:

Therefore, as the elect of God, holy and beloved, put on tender mercies, kindness, humility, meekness, longsuffering; bearing with one another, and forgiving one another, if anyone has a complaint against another; even as Christ forgave you, so you also must do. But above all these things put on love, which is the bond of perfection. And let the peace of God rule in your hearts, to which also you were called in one body; and be thankful. Let the word of Christ dwell in you richly in all wisdom, teaching and admonishing one another in psalms and hymns and spiritual songs, singing with grace in your hearts to the Lord. And whatever you do in word or deed, do all in the name of the Lord Jesus, giving thanks to God the Father through Him.

It starts with being made new in Christ (verse 10).

It adds to that, living a life of holiness, humbleness, meekness, patience, forgiveness, and love. Don't face the upcoming winter without being prepared, wasting precious time adding items to the food pile that will never see you through the winter.

Image

A famous tennis player had some commercials where he claimed "image is everything." Experience tells us otherwise. While image may indeed give us a clue as to what to expect from a given person, the actions of the person usually either confirm or deny the expectations. Sometimes images are made to show a picture or profile of people and places. Pull out a coin and look at the image of a former President. While you may never have met Mr. Jefferson, chances are you know what his image looks like. What a disappointment if President Jefferson showed up in person, alive and well in Washington D.C., and he looked nothing like his image.

That brings me to the bachelor beaver. Now the name itself may or may not be found in the scientific realm of beaver studies, but a veteran trapper, who has waded many a swamp with me, calls them by that name. It seems to fit. Beavers for the most part are one big, happy family. They roam the creeks and rivers seeking culverts, ditches, and any forestry operation that might allow them to practice their mystic arts. A mystic art like damming those streams and ditches in just the right place, to cause maximum flooding; or placing a dam within the one culvert that is the hardest to reach into.

But all is not always happy in the lodge. It seems that the females will on occasion kick out the oldest male. Biologists do not know why, but theories abound: poor hygiene, leaving chips and splinters on the couch, tracking mud throughout the freshly cleaned lodge, or watching TV instead of gathering supplies for the winter. These are some of the leading causes listed by pollsters. Regardless of the reason, it seems that a lone beaver will often have to vacate the lodge and take up residence by himself.

The bachelor beaver is often a ghost. He never does things you expect him to do. He never seems to follow the right paths; he might disappear for days, and generally refuses to be trapped. He even seems reluctant to tend to his dam, which is always a prerequisite for a beaver. But the area gives unmistakable signs that a beaver is present. Gnawed sticks floating in the water, dams, trees that have lost bark, and muddy footprints—all point to the fact that a beaver is present.

As it is required of me to remove many beavers that seek to reside on the lands that I manage, it is a source of disappointment when I realize after several trapping scenarios, that I am dealing with a bachelor beaver. You see, a beaver should act like a beaver. The signs tell me that he is there, but his behavior would seem to indicate that he has left the area. He stays in holes and old stumps instead of lodges, and will often let you drain his pond without repairing his dam nightly. He will make you question his existence, and cause you to leave the area convinced that he has left; only to come out of hiding and again flood your property.

In Genesis, we are told that we are made in the image of God.

Genesis 1:27 *So God created man in His own image; in the image of God He created him; male and female He created them.*

That means we have something in common with God. Through our lives, through our existence, we have the ability to show others what God is like. We have the capacity to love, to embrace, to plan, to manage, to express emotion. We can think and then act upon those thoughts in acts of pre-meditation. We can exercise free will. All of this sets us apart from the animal kingdom. In this our Creator has taken a huge risk. He has allowed His creation to be an expression of Himself. To prove His existence, we are forced to look at the images He has placed on this earth to represent Him.

In II Corinthians 4:11, Paul informs Christians that their calling is to make Jesus manifested in their lives, to make their lives appear to others like the image of Jesus:

For we who live are always delivered to death for Jesus' sake, that the life of Jesus also may be manifested in our mortal flesh.

How do we accomplish this task? What is it that we are to show to others?

John 3:16 *"For God so loved the world..."* We are to show the image of love.

Romans 5:6b *...Christ died for the ungodly.* We are to show the image of sacrifice.

I John 1:9: *...He is faithful and just to forgive us...* We are to show the image of forgiveness.

Like a bachelor beaver, Christians are often guilty of not acting "like Christ." We leave signs all around us by going to church, participating in activities, singing in the choir. We give every indication that we are faithful; until someone comes looking for us, looking for an image of God. They are looking for love, sacrifice, forgiveness. Unfortunately, Christians often are guilty of going into hiding. We choose not to show the image of the one who created us for that very purpose. Tragically, we refuse to come out; we refuse to engage others who are in need. We find the solitude of our little pond to be best when we alone are in it. What a disappointment it must be for the Creator who has invested and entrusted us to represent Him.

A neighbor sits by the phone, alone. A widow, she sits waiting for the doctor's office to call with the test results. She expects the worse; she would love to have had her husband there to comfort her, or a child, or a friend. But it seems no one has time. No one is available to share a hand or lend an ear, to be at her side when the call comes in. God wants to be there. He can hold her heart, but He needs us to hold her hand, to be the image of His compassion.

What a waste. A life lived in the streets. Their past is littered with failures and abuses. They once had a future, a family, a job. They had respect and purpose. Then they made a wrong turn; took some wrong advice; chose the wrong friends. Now they are caught in an endless cycle of defeat. Satan laughs. How easy it is to capture us by our deceit, our belief that alone we have the strength to withstand him. Our belief that those who fail and fall should be left to reap what they have sown. May God forgive us of our vanity! Jesus came to die for the ungodly. He referred to the religious leaders of His day as decaying and rotting corpses. He showed them sacrifice, His own life in exchange for their sins. What do we do? How much of a sacrifice do we make for those who are locked in mortal combat with Satan? God offers salvation, hope, and a future, but He needs a messenger.

Bitterness: like a cancer it eats away at us. We say we forgive, but we never forget. We hold it for the next argument, to be used like a secret weapon. We throw it in the face of our spouses, our parents, our children, and our friends. We never let them forget how they have hurt us. But God forgives and forgets. Nothing is worth the pain of separation to God. He sent His Son to die for all of our sins, because of His great love. God wants to heal our bitterness, to teach us that nothing is worse than being separated from Him. He needs Christians to be the advertisement; to show that the product works. We endorse it, but do we use it?

Image is everything. Perhaps the commercial had it right after all. How can we believe in a God whom we cannot see, if those who claim to represent Him are more interested in running away from Him then they are in serving Him? Don't be guilty of hiding the image. Let it shine forth, regardless of the cost. Jesus will show up one day very soon. We need to know what he will look like now.

Foresters and Fishing

Foresters and fishing seem to go hand in hand. Many, if not all of the foresters I know, are habitual fisherman. They are often exposed to the incredible temptation of being invited to fish those farm ponds across the field, next to the farmers forty acres of timber that he is planning to sell.

Usually the day goes like this. You have received a call from Farmer Brown, who wants to sell forty acres of pine and hardwood timber on the southwest corner of his property. You arrive bright and early the next day, ready to tackle the cruise, and hopefully close the deal before competing foresters in the area can show up and offer a counter-offer. As you drive onto the farm, you notice the timber off in the distance, tall and mature. Your excitement builds at the idea of cruising through a fine stand of trees. Then you notice a willow tree. A willow tree on a farm usually means one thing—a pond. Ponds on farms bring up ideas of massive amounts of fish, fish that have never seen a lure or hook.

As the farmer tells you about his woods, explains the locations of his corners and lines, and mentions about the hostile bull that roams the east side of the farm—you are already sorting lures in your mind. Visions of being a TV fisherman, explaining to the audience how a lure is supposed to work as you pull in yet another massive bass, have caused your eyes to go blank, and small amounts of drool to gather at the corners of your mouth. Finally Farmer Brown concludes with, "Any questions?" You casually ask about the pond. "Help yourself," he replies, and your day is complete, even your week.

Foresters will volunteer to work Saturdays and holidays, checking on the condition of a tract of timber daily, if fishing is involved. They use excuses such as guarding against southern pine beetles that might come in and attack the forest; or they explain to their boss they are looking for "signs of competitors" who might be trying to buy the timber for another mill. Now their boss believes these signs of competition to be paint or flagging in the woods, footprints, or fresh tire tracks; and that any of these would show that competing mills are looking at the timber. However, the forester is actually watching the pond, looking for snagged lures, footprints, or forked sticks. This is the competition that concerns him most. Often the forester will state that they need to get the layout of the tract in their minds better so they can get the logging job started out in the right place, but they are trying to find out where the bream beds are, and if catfish or bass are present.

But often the pond is nothing but a puddle of water, a means of capturing rainwater to irrigate a field. It looks fishy, and certainly has the snakes and frogs necessary for any southern pond, but it has never been stocked. It is just a puddle. That is usually what I find when I attempt to fish any pond. It is just a puddle, or at least I never catch anything to prove otherwise.

Not catching anything brings us to Luke 5, and a fishing story. Jesus is strolling through the country, speaking and healing folks as He goes. Soon the crowd is so great that Jesus is forced up against a lake, referred to as the Lake of Gennesaret in verse 1. As He has run out of dry real estate, the next message must either be taught while in the water, or on top of the water. He calls for a boat.

Meanwhile, Peter and his fellow fishermen are off to the side cleaning nets. It must be understood that Peter was a professional fisherman. He made his living on the water. Verse 5 informs us that the men had been out all night fishing, a necessity in that land due to the heat of the day. Fish stayed away during the day. Apparently, they stayed away that night also, as Peter later informs us. Jesus requests a boat, which Peter supplies—anything to get out of cleaning nets and being reminded of a long-wasted night of labor. It is after the sermon that things get interesting.

Luke 5:4 *When He had stopped speaking, He said to Simon, "Launch out into the deep and let down your nets for a catch."*

Maybe Jesus was getting in over His head. He was seeking to instruct a professional fisherman on how and when to fish. Hello, it is daytime and hot? Fish bite in the night...well for most folks...Peter is quick to point this out. Thus, faced with the option of fishing or working, or the choice of fishing versus mending the nets, it really was a no brainer, "Let's fish!" Peter gives the nets a toss and his life changes forever.

Luke 5:5 *But Simon answered and said to Him, "Master, we have toiled all night and caught nothing; nevertheless at Your word I will let down the net."*

Up until now, Peter was fishing in an un-stocked pond so to speak. He couldn't prove the lake held anything. But something was about to happen that changed Peter's life. He got a bite. Verse six tells us that suddenly fish, apparently from the entire lake, began fighting to get into the nets. Against all natural patterns, the nets were being quickly filled with fish. Nets started to break, and boats began to sink. They called for their partners, who came and quickly had their boats swamped with fish. Standing there, amidst a boat slowly sinking under the ever-growing pile of fish, Peter drops to his knees in front of Jesus.

Luke 5: 8 *When Simon Peter saw it, he fell down at Jesus' knees, saying, "Depart from me, for I am a sinful man, O Lord!"*

Did you ever wonder how Jesus would answer that question if it were you? Peter did not beg for mercy. He knew he was in the presence of God, and he knew he did not deserve to be there. The true miracle of this story is not in the fish being caught, but that Jesus loves us. We have nothing to offer Him. He has everything to offer to us.

Perhaps the most intriguing verse of this story is in the ending.

Luke 5:11 *So when they had brought their boats to land, they forsook all and followed Him.*

They were fishermen, men who made their living on the water catching fish. They were looking at money, wealth, and reputation, all in those two boats overflowing with fish. And Jesus was offering them something else. As if to say to them, "What is so special about what you do for a living? To be sure you want more out of life then a boat full of fish. When these fish are gone, what then? You must again cast the nets. Is that what you want, the endless repetition of pursuing wealth and fame. Instead, let me be your living, let me be the reason you get up in the morning, and I will show you the true meaning of life." Jesus calls us to fall on our knees, to understand that He alone holds the truth, the way to life eternal.

John 14:6 *Jesus said to him, "I am the way, the truth, and the life. No one comes to the Father except through Me."*

Don't get caught standing beside the boat and not following Jesus. It is hot by the boat, and it is full of fish. Jesus offers us something better.

Marking the Boundaries

If you have ever driven down a road in the South, you have probably noticed trees along the highway, and in particular, trees with bands of paint on them. These trees have been painted with a purpose, and that purpose is to show where a particular property's boundary line is. You see, tracts of land larger than your average house lot are often places of great activity such as timber harvesting, planting, hunting, or road construction. The owners of these properties, usually timber companies, mark their property lines in order to keep their personnel and contractors on the right property.

For example, you told your logger to cut until he came to the, "end of the pines." If you gave those simple instructions to a logger while standing anywhere in Georgia, he might cut until he hit saltwater. Instead, you would tell him to cut until he comes to the, "line of trees banded with yellow paint." If you had marked the trees at the end of your property with yellow paint, then that is where he would stop cutting.

These lines also serve as a means of distinguishing one owner from another. Some companies use yellow, some blue or orange, and they seek to be consistent. This allows local folks at the corner hardware store to know whose land is on fire.

"Say Bill, who is it that owns the timberlands marked in red, cause there's a fire up there that's not to be believed. Maybe we should call them as soon as we finish this game of checkers."

However, the number one purpose of the boundary line is to show where the ownership starts and stops, and it is supposed to be exactly the description that is found in the local county courthouse. Yes the local county court house, where myth and legality intertwine. There is no telling what you might find after spending a day researching old deeds and papers. Some properties rarely change hands, thus their deed descriptions might go back into past centuries. That is to say exactly the description as written by a surveyor named George Washington. Yes once a property is measured, then it seems no one ever wants to bring it up to date, so the original description always seems to stay. For example, you are looking for the lines to Mr. Smith's property, which he has owned for twenty years. He bought it from Daniel Boone, who bought it from Noah. The description goes like this:

"Take ye two score paces due north until ye come to an apple tree planted by Abraham's wife. Turn north by northwest, and proceed along the run of Fillmore Creek until you come to the stump where Miles Standish ate lunch in 1492, and turn south. Travel to the intersection of the pathway used by Geronimo, and turn east until you come to the place you started from."

The surveyor is responsible for all of this. He walks the line as it is agreed to and writes down a course of direction, noting landmarks and compass bearings. As he travels, he marks the trees with a hatchet or machete, leaving a chopped mark in the bark. This mark will remain for as long as the tree lives, or until you are the one trying to follow the line through the woods and you need to find these marks.

Thus the work of the surveyor is of utmost importance to the landowner. He sets the boundary line; the line where ownerships change, the line where the nature of the work changes, the line that reminds the passerby that they have entered onto another's property. The boundary line is the most important landmark in the woods. The forester's job often calls for him to make sure these marks can be seen, to clear away brush and vines, and add new paint as the old paint fades. Neglecting the boundary lines can cause great headaches down the road. Loggers cut the wrong timber; no one knows who to call when a fire breaks out; or someone buys the wrong land.

Landmarks are not new. They have been in use since time began. They set boundaries and remind folks of who owned what. Joshua, as he was leading the children of Israel into the Promised Land, felt inclined to set up a landmark. They were crossing the Jordan, and once again God had caused the water to part, and allowed the people to cross the river on dry ground.

Joshua 4: 19-24 *Now the people came up from the Jordan on the tenth day of the first month, and they camped in Gilgal on the east border of Jericho. And those twelve stones which they took out of the Jordan, Joshua set up in Gilgal. Then he spoke to the children of Israel, saying: "When your children ask their fathers in time to come, saying, 'What are these stones?' then you shall let your children know, saying, 'Israel crossed over this Jordan on dry land'; for the LORD your God dried up the waters of the Jordan before you until you had crossed over, as the LORD your God did to the Red Sea, which He dried up before us until we had crossed over, that all the peoples of the earth may know the hand of the LORD, that it is mighty, that you may fear the LORD your God forever."*

Joshua was just stepping foot onto the land that God had promised His people. He immediately set a landmark, a boundary marker if you will, because it would be there to remind Israel that God fulfills His promises. It would serve to remind them that God had delivered them in the past, and that He would deliver them in the future. But did you notice whom it was for? It was for the future generations. He had crossed the river and the sea on dry ground, He had seen the waters rise up, and had walked under the shadow of the waves. He had seen God work first hand. Future generations were relying upon these folks to show them and tell them about God's great acts.

Now the bad news:

Judges 2:8 *Now Joshua the son of Nun, the servant of the Lord, died when he was one hundred and ten years old.*

More bad news:

Judges 2:10 *When all that generation had been gathered to their fathers, another generation arose after them who did not know the LORD nor the work which He had done for Israel.*

Even more bad news:

BIBLES, BEAVERS, AND BIG TIMBER

Judges 2:11 Then the children of Israel did evil in the sight of the Lord...

The generation had failed to pass it on. They had failed to influence their children with the importance of following God. Without boundaries, without landmarks, the children wandered, they became lost, and they forgot God. They never knew that they had value, that God wanted to love them and protect them; that He wanted to lead them to a life full of promise. They never heard it.

It is vital that those around us know what we stand for. That they know we are owned by someone different. Christians do not belong to the ruler of this world, they belong to God. The shed blood of Jesus purchased them. The ownership changed. Our boundary should be clearly marked. Those that approach us, who work with us, who are members of our family, should see the line clearly. The paint should stand out. And when others ask, when the children come to us and say, "Why do you believe there is a God?" Then be ready with an answer—be ready to share with them that Jesus paid for your sins by dying on the cross in your place. And He has marked us, to show others that there is a better way, a way of peace and joy that can only be found in Christ.

The Apostle Paul calls for us to be different, to be separated from the world, to show that we are under new ownership.

Romans 12:2 And do not be conformed to this world, but be transformed by the renewing of your mind, that you may prove what is that good and acceptable and perfect will of God.

How are your landmarks?

Proverbs 22:28 Do not remove the ancient landmark which your fathers have set.

The Pickle Bucket of Grace

Fire and forestry have long had a love/hate relationship. Talk to Smokey Bear about the "hate side." On the "love side" is the land management forester. Fire, in the form of a "controlled burn," is used by foresters to prepare areas for planting or to remove excess debris that could ignite at the wrong time and cause serious damage. Burning opportunities are always an adventure. To have a happy, joyous burning experience, follow these directions:

Step 1) Determine wind direction and speed.

Step 2) Allow the area to be burned to dry-out, to the point where just thinking about lighting a match will cause smoke.

Step 3) Set several things of importance on your schedule to be completed the day of your burn, but schedule them for after your burn

Step 4) Verify that your cell phone has no service or coverage.

Step 5) Light the fire as a backfire, meaning the wind will push against it and allow for a slow, controlled fire.

Step 6) Run as the wind changes 180 degrees and backfire becomes head fire; meaning the wind is pushing it and it is fast and out of control...and probably headed for your truck.

Anyone who has been involved in a controlled burn has experienced the above formula to one degree or another. The wind changes, intensifies, and the tract that was thought to be too wet to burn lights up like Atlanta when Sherman came for a visit. When all the conditions are just right for a burn, it is usually not the time to burn. Fire seems to make its own rules.

I was burning-off an old log deck one morning. (A log deck usually is littered with chunks of wood that were defective and hollow, and could not be salvaged. A large pile of wood is what we are talking about here.) The breeze was just right; it was late spring and things were greening up. The pile was at the edge of a large cutover which was surrounded by a pond, a plowed field, and a major river. The tract, which the logger had finished several months before, had already been planted; and I was just looking to clean up the deck area that was rather unsightly. The weather over the winter had not allowed us to do a site prep burn; and rather than miss a planting season, we decided to plant it as it was. No sooner had I started burning, than the breeze shifted to a hard gale. It seemed that a low off the coast had backed in faster than the weather folks had anticipated. My deck fire began to "spot" out in the cutover, 100 yards from the deck, which was well past the bare dirt, fire lines that I had surrounded it with. Soon, I had fire everywhere.

The problem that I had not anticipated, that of a deck fire jumping a road and fire lines, suddenly changed the nature of my day. The wind was so intense that fires were breaking out everywhere. It did not seem to be even remotely containable. Was a river 80 yards wide going to stop a fire already jumping 100 yards? Everything that seemed to be so controlled was now in chaos. I proceeded to Step 4. After climbing up on several different stumps, I finally found one that allowed me to pick up one signal bar on my cell phone. After consulting with the Forest Service, getting a revised weather forecast and requesting a tractor, it was time to get to work.

When I first started in forestry, the paper company I worked for requested that I live in a certain section of the county, as that would allow me to be available to respond to forest fires in that area on company property. This meant calling for tractors and the local VFD, as well as leading these crews onto the property to fight the fires. But they also asked me to carry something in my truck to help—a pickle bucket. Yes, a five gallon plastic bucket, the kind restaurants purchase pickles in. You can also get five gallon buckets of dry wall mud, or hydraulic fuel buckets, but I have always preferred pickle buckets. We were supposed to keep one in our trucks in the event that fires jumped roads or fire lanes. Every road or lane had a ditch;

and ditches have water; and fires hate water. Fill the bucket, pour the bucket and repeat.

Thus, out of the back of my Chevy Blazer, came the pickle bucket. It was full of chains, paint cans, and flashlights; but soon it was empty, and ready for service. Now the pickle bucket does not come with many accessories, usually just a handle, and if you're lucky, maybe the handle is form-fitted instead of just a round tube. All I needed now was water, and I had a whole river to use. My goal was to stop the spot-overs. Spot-overs are the new fires that are being formed by sparks blowing from the original fire. Usually these are across the property where we do not want fire. If the property next to the area you want to burn is your company's, rest easy the fire won't go there! Spot-overs have a sadistic yearning for new property, especially property not owned by those doing the burning. If the wind isn't blowing that way when you start, don't worry, it will. If you can get to them fast enough, usually one good bucket can drench the flames, and thus keep the fire from getting larger.

Now the thing about fire is this; give it wind and it will burn until it has no more fuel to burn. The hotter the fire, the more strength it has. And on that day my fire was getting hotter by the minute. Upon his arrival, the man from the Forest Service echoed my thoughts: "It will burn, and it will jump, we can just hope that it doesn't jump the river, because in this wind, no six-foot fire line is going to stop it."

It was during this day of toting water that I saw a picture of grace. As I mentioned earlier, most of the area had been freshly planted with new pine seedlings. On one of the spot-overs, one of my seedlings was being surrounded by fire. By instinct I immediately poured my bucket around the seedling. Many of the planted pines had already gone up in small puffs of smoke, but I was all for saving what I could. I had already invested money in those trees. I went back and checked on that tree throughout the day, and was pleased to see it had not been scorched. All day as I ran after spots, I looked first for the seedling, making sure I drenched it with water—water that would save it from the advancing flames.

Isaiah 10:16-19 *Therefore the Lord, the Lord of hosts, will send leanness among his fat ones; and under his glory He will kindle a burning like the burning of a fire. So the Light of Israel will be for a fire, and his Holy One for a flame; it will burn and devour his thorns and his briers in one day. And it will consume the glory of his forest and of his fruitful field, both soul and body; and they will be as when a sick man wastes away. Then the rest of the trees of his forest will be so few in number that a child may write them.*

The trees unburned in this passage refer to the "remnant," those that remained faithful, those that God had chosen to protect, that he had showed grace to. The Apostle Paul said it like this:

Romans 11:5,6 *Even so then, at this present time there is a remnant according to the election of grace. And if by grace, then it is no longer of works; otherwise grace is no longer grace. But if it is of works, it is no longer grace; otherwise work is no longer work.*

Have you got the picture yet? We are those seedlings. Each one rooted in the earth, unable to move, there is no "work" that we can do. We are small and defenseless in the face of an approaching fire. That fire is coming; it is the wrath of God on sinful man. He is judging, and His judgment is sure. There is no escaping it. We cannot run from it, nor can we resist it. Then through the smoke comes Jesus, carrying a pickle bucket in his nail-scarred hands. It is full of the water of his grace. He offers to us this living water:

John 4:10 *Jesus answered and said to her, "If you knew the gift of God, and who it is who says to you, 'Give Me a drink,' you would have asked Him, and He would have given you living water."*

He is offering us a way to escape the flames. How do we respond?

"Leave the bucket here. I will pour it when I start getting hot."

"I would rather enjoy the warm weather."

"I just did my hair, and I don't think the fire will really come this way."

"I am tough, I will survive."

It is indeed tragic that we respond with such ignorance; with such bravado, and such carelessness.

Salvation is by grace and grace alone. There is no part that we can play in it, except surrendering and begging for the water of grace to be poured out. And we need to allow Christ to cover us with the living water, water that was purchased on Calvary.

Where do you stand today? It's pretty dry out, the wind is blowing, and I smell smoke...

The Ride Home

Throughout this book we have mentioned the "truck." The truck is really an office on wheels for the forester. It contains maps of timber sales past and present, and road maps that are actually consulted. You will find electronic gear of all kinds, from laptop computers to hand held computers, to GPS receivers, to CB radios and cell phones. There are enough pens and pencils to furnish a grade school for a year, and paperclips and probably a miniature stapler in the glove box with all of the keys. There are more keys than can be counted, usually with no labels at all on them. The keys are for gates, gates with locks that have to be matched to the keys—in a weird, lottery sort of way, until the right key is found.

Clothes can also be found in the truck. It is sort of like a rummage sale with old tattered shirts and briar pants, and some socks. There are boots of every shape and size: snake boots, hips boots, work boots, and mud boots. One can also find the tools of the trade in the truck such as: diameter tapes for measuring trees, ribbon flagging for marking lines, paint cans and paint guns, bug juice (insect repellant), and an old orange cruising vest, splattered with paint from every color of the spectrum. This vest carries enough fumes to kill plant life and small rodents as the forester walks by; but strangely enough the forester's sense of smell has been warped over the years, and he actually likes the smell of Deep Woods OFF.

It is the passenger seat that is truly unique about the forester's truck. Most foresters spend a great deal of their time alone, and on the road. The passenger seat holds all the important items for the day ahead. There is an appointment book opened to today, a list of important phone numbers, and maps of where in the world today's adventure is supposed to begin. And of course, breakfast, or lunch recently purchased at the local gas station. As each task is completed during the day, as messages are collected from phone calls, timber sales won or lost, fast food consumed—the passenger side floorboard becomes the trashcan. When asked to hop into the truck with a forester, you must give him a few minutes to clean his office, by which he means the seat. Necessary things are moved, the rest is swept to the floor. As the passenger, you can just hop on the seat and place your feet on the trash, and buckle up!

Few things can ruin a forester's day like having his truck in the shop. He is lost—wandering around the office, eating "nabs" from the vending machine. Like Linus and his blanket, so are a forester and his truck. Thus it is with little surprise, that at the end of a long day in the woods—when we are crawling out of the swamp, drained of our last ounce of blood from the horde of still circling mosquitoes; bites from where the yellow flies were drilling into our hands; water sloshing about in our boots; and our stomach still in knots from that potted meat we bought at the gas station—we see our truck and we rejoice. We know we have survived another day in the woods, and that home is waiting. We turn on the air conditioner, kill a dozen flies and mosquitoes that came in when we opened the door, pull off our wet boots, and sigh. In our pocket we have the completed cruise, or field notes, or the satisfaction of knowing we completed the mission for today. Making it back to the truck insures us that we will not die in the swamp and that our body can more easily be found. It means the day was successful.

The Apostle Paul knew what it was like:

2 Timothy 4:6-8 For I am already being poured out as a drink offering, and the time of my departure is at hand. I have fought the good fight, I have finished the race, I have kept the faith. Finally, there is laid up for me the crown of righteousness, which the Lord, the righteous Judge, will give to me on that Day, and not to me only but also to all who have loved His appearing.

Each of us will come to a time, a time to get into the truck. The course that was set before us has been completed. It will not matter then what tracts of timber we bought or didn't buy, or how many beavers we removed, or how many games of checkers we won at the local hardware store. What will matter is what we did with

BIBLES, BEAVERS, AND BIG TIMBER

Jesus: Jesus, the ultimate forester! He would have no problem with tree identification, and He would be a master with a compass. Jesus would be ready to break a path for us, to absorb the painful stings and briars; a hand to pull us out of a hole; a friend; a Savior.

Revelation 3:20 *"Behold, I stand at the door and knock. If anyone hears My voice and opens the door, I will come in to him and dine with him, and he with Me."*

How about it? The ride home would be better with someone in the truck with you. Clean off the passenger seat, and slide over. Let Jesus take the wheel, and make your life successful.